GLOBALIZATION AND MILITARISM

GLOBALIZATION

Series Editors

Manfred B. Steger

*Royal Melbourne Institute of Technology
and University of Hawai'i–Mānoa*

and

Terrell Carver

University of Bristol

"Globalization" has become *the* buzzword of our time. But what does it mean? Rather than forcing a complicated social phenomenon into a single analytical framework, this series seeks to present globalization as a multidimensional process constituted by complex, often contradictory interactions of global, regional, and local aspects of social life. Since conventional disciplinary borders and lines of demarcation are losing their old rationales in a globalizing world, authors in this series apply an interdisciplinary framework to the study of globalization. In short, the main purpose and objective of this series is to support subject-specific inquiries into the dynamics and effects of contemporary globalization and its varying impacts across, between, and within societies.

Globalization and Sovereignty
John Agnew

Globalization and War
Tarak Barkawi

Globalization and Human Security
Paul Battersby and Joseph M. Siracusa

Globalization and the Environment
Peter Christoff and Robyn Eckersley

Globalization and American Popular Culture, 3rd ed.
Lane Crothers

Globalization and Militarism
Cynthia Enloe

Globalization and Law
Adam Gearey

Globalization and Feminist Activism
Mary E. Hawkesworth

Globalization and Postcolonialism
Sankaran Krishna

Globalization and Media
Jack Lule

Globalization and Social Movements, 2nd ed.
Valentine M. Moghadam

Globalization and Terrorism, 2nd ed.
Jamal R. Nassar

Globalization and Culture, 3rd ed.
Jan Nederveen Pieterse

Globalization and Democracy
Stephen J. Rosow and Jim George

Globalization and International Political Economy
Mark Rupert and M. Scott Solomon

Globalization and Citizenship
Hans Schattle

Globalization and Money
Supriya Singh

Globalization and Islamism
Nevzat Soguk

Globalization and Urbanization
James H. Spencer

Globalisms, 3rd ed.
Manfred B. Steger

Rethinking Globalism
Edited by Manfred B. Steger

Globalization and Labor
Dimitris Stevis and Terry Boswell

Globaloney 2.0
Michael Veseth

Supported by the Globalization Research Center at the University of Hawai'i, Mānoa

GLOBALIZATION AND MILITARISM

FEMINISTS MAKE THE LINK

SECOND EDITION

CYNTHIA ENLOE

ROWMAN & LITTLEFIELD
Lanham • Boulder • New York • London

Published by Rowman & Littlefield
A wholly owned subsidiary of The Rowman & Littlefield Publishing Group, Inc.
4501 Forbes Boulevard, Suite 200, Lanham, Maryland 20706
www.rowman.com

Unit A, Whitacre Mews, 26-34 Stannary Street, London SE11 4AB, United Kingdom

Some material in chapters 3, 4, 5, and 8 was originally translated into Japanese by
Kozue Akibayashi, edited by the Ochanomizu University Institute for Gender Studies,
and published by Ochanomizu Shobo, Publishers, under the title *Exploring Militarism
and International Politics with a Feminist Curiosity* (2004), by Cynthia Enloe.

An earlier, quite different, version of chapter 6 was published as: "Wielding
Masculinity Inside Abu Ghraib," *Asian Journal of Women's Studies* 10, no. 3
(September 2004): 235–243.

British Library Cataloguing in Publication Information Available

Library of Congress Cataloging-in-Publication Data

Names: Enloe, Cynthia H., 1938– author.
Title: Globalization and militarism : feminists make the link / Cynthia Enloe.
Description: Second edition. | Lanham : Rowman & Littlefield, [2016] |
  Series: Globalization | Includes bibliographical references and index.
Identifiers: LCCN 2016000792 (print) | LCCN 2016002096 (ebook) |
  ISBN 9781442265431 (cloth : alk. paper) | ISBN 9781442265448
  (pbk. : alk. paper) | ISBN 9781442265455 (electronic)
Subjects: LCSH: Globalization. | Militarism. | Women and the military. |
  Women soldiers. | Disarmament.
Classification: LCC JZ1318 .E65 2016 (print) | LCC JZ1318 (ebook) | DDC
  303.48/2—dc22
LC record available at http://lccn.loc.gov/2016000792

Printed in the United States of America

This book is dedicated to

Ann, Spike, Jindy, Sandy, Marysia, Anne, Gillian, Kathy, Jane, Marianne, Judith, Kathy, Christine, Francine, Laura, Shirin, Susan, Cyndy, Lily, Terrell, Laura, Mary, Lisa, Aaron, Jacqui, Megan, Maya, Catia, Caron, Denise, Jill, Carol, Laura, Catherine, Deborah, Judith, Annica, Rekha, Meredith, Simona, Annick, Victoria, Dan, Kristen, Paul, Sandy, Inger, Torunn, Swati, Fumika, and all of the smart, energetic feminist scholars who are transforming International Relations.

CONTENTS

PREFACE TO THE
SECOND EDITION

Everyone who ever writes a book—or an article, term paper, blog, or script—is writing in the midst of history. That is, each of us is always writing within a particular swirl of events, relationships, ideas, and unnoticed trends. Recognizing this does not mean that one's writings are instantly "out-of-date"; instead, it enriches one's writings. More important, being historically aware of one's place in history will enrich the experience of those reading one's writings. Hiding those circumstances is a disservice to readers.

I am sitting down to write this new edition of *Globalization and Militarism* at a distinctive time in the ongoing gendered developments of globalization, of militarism, and of feminism. This is a time in world history that seems hyper-militarized, with civilians in allegedly peaceful countries fearing not just acts of terror, but whole categories of people whom they imagine to be threats. It is a time when armed conflicts are raging on the ground and from the skies in myriad regions, forcing hundreds of thousands of women and men to embark on dangerous journeys to escape that violence in leaky boats and on blistered feet.

This is a time when some societies are remaining stubbornly militarized: for instance, Russia, the United States, Sudan, Israel, Egypt, Syria, Afghanistan, Iraq, and India. It is a time when other societies are rapidly militarizing or remilitarizing: for instance, Turkey, Japan, Saudi Arabia, United Arab Emirates, Yemen, Djibouti, China, Mexico, and France. Simultaneously, however, this is a time when some societies are taking notable, if halting, collective steps toward *de*-militarization: Myanmar

(Burma), Colombia, Canada, and Indonesia. Among the world's least militarized nations today are Iceland, Costa Rica, and Samoa.

This is a time too, however, when more and more people in each of these gross societal categories are talking with each other about the possible connections between globalizing dynamics, militarism's beliefs and values, and the complex ideas that propel feminism.

For instance, today more people than ever are asking: Is feminism becoming genuinely globalized, or is it still an essentially locally rooted, merely a cultural-bound set of ideas? Similarly, more people than ever are asking: Is militarism becoming globalized so rampantly that those who have garnered crucial lessons from successful peace-building can scarcely keep up? And, linking these two questions: Can any society successfully reverse militarizing dynamics if it does not take seriously the workings of patriarchy?

In my writing this new edition and your reading it, we together are joining a global conversation. We didn't start the conversation, and we won't end it. It is a conversation that is intense because its substance matters. If we lazily ask simplistic questions or draw self-serving conclusions, we will jeopardize the lives of women and men whom we hardly know.

ACKNOWLEDGMENTS

The early seeds for this book were planted in a series of lectures sponsored by Ochanomizu University in Tokyo. It was during a tense time, on the verge of the March 2003 U.S.-led invasion of Iraq. Many Japanese were intently following the UN debates and the military buildup. The Japanese usually keep a close eye on the United States—its styles, its movies, its economy, its politics, its sports (while I was there, Ichiro Suzuki's performance in spring training with the Seattle Mariners was the topic of daily coverage, and Michael Moore's film "Bowling for Columbine" was drawing large audiences in movie theaters around the country). But in the early months of 2003, many Japanese were particularly worried that Washington would pressure Japanese officials to make at least a token gesture of military involvement in the United States' invasion of Iraq—despite the Japanese constitution, which forbids any Japanese military involvement in aggressive operations.

The Tokyo organizers were the faculty of Institute for Gender Studies at Ochanomizu University, one of Japan's premier centers for women's studies teaching and research. The eighty or so people who came to each talk held at this famous national women's university were drawn by a desire to make sense of complex international politics, combined with an interest in exploring the ways that feminist analysis might shed light on international politics.

I learned a great deal from preparing those talks (for instance, trying to make sure that I didn't fall into any U.S.-centric assumptions) and especially, from taking part in the lively discussions that followed each talk, first in the large auditorium and then over red wine and sand-wiches at the Institute for Gender Studies' crowded offices across campus. It was a wonderful three months.

The first version of this book was influenced by being crafted during the international wars in Afghanistan and Iraq and during the years marked by local and international efforts to end wars in the former Yugoslavia, Israel, Lebanon, Palestine, Chechnya, Congo, Liberia, Sierra Leone, Sudan, East Timor, Nepal, and Sri Lanka. Only some of those efforts—attempts to globalize *de*militarization—have proved even par-tially successful. But every one of those efforts has generated fresh insights.

I remain in debt to all the researchers and activists who did this important work during these years, as well as to all of those who have picked up the baton and continued to dig, and ponder, and then dig some more. They have come from dozens of countries. It is impossible to get a realistic grip on intersecting militarizing and globalizing pro-cesses if one listens to, or reads, only observers coming from a handful of societies. As you read the chapters ahead, imagine me listening to Canadian feminists discussing the still-masculinized politics of their own country's much-praised UN peacekeeping operations; picture me sitting at a café poring over the latest reports published by the Belgrade Women in Black peace activists; think of me reading and then rereading letters, clippings, and e-mails from researchers and activist friends in Tel Aviv, Istanbul, Santiago, Boston, Philadelphia, Tokyo, Oslo, Stock-holm, Geneva, Toronto, London, Auckland, Dublin, Brighton, Johan-nesburg, Seoul, and Bogota. I have sought here to do justice to all of their insights.

My special thanks go to all the members of the wonderful Feminist Theory and Gender Section ("FTGS") of the International Studies Association, to whom this book is dedicated. More thanks go to my tutors Ayse Gul Altinay, Rela Mezali, Madeleine Rees, Ann Tickner, Sandra Harding, Ruri Ito, Tanya Henderson, Maya Eichler, Lisa Prugl, Orna Sasson-Levy, Lena Ag, Ariane Brunet, Jane Parpart, Lois Wasser-spring, Lepa Mladjenovic, Stasa Zajovic, Ximena Bunster, Ailbhe Smyth, Christine Ahn, Insook Kwon, Parissara (Gai) Liewkeat, Sandra McEvoy, Gyoungsun Jang, Laura Hammond, Michele Fillion, Michelle Morkert, Nadje Al-Ali, Maja Korac, Amrita Basu, Mary Katzenstein, Martha Ack-elsberg, Molly Shanley, Eileen McDonagh, and the late Rita Arditti.

My warm thanks too to Elora Chowdhury, Cynthia Cockburn, Carol Cohn, Annica Kronsell, Adriana Benjumea, Carla Afonso, Laura Mitchell, Nhung Dinh, Helga Hermes, Inger Skjelsbaek, Torunn Tryggestad, Catia Confortini, Marsha Henry, Vron Ware, Denise Bebbington, Anita Fabos, Kristen Williams, Valerie Sperling, Dan Conway, Jef Huysmans, the late Saralee Hamilton, Felicity Hill, Nadine Puechguirbal, Aaron Belkin, Teresia Teaiwa, Anita Lacey, Tom Gregory, Sohaila Abdulali, Abigail Disney, Paul Higate, Nishkala Suntharlingam, Aakriti Pandey, Victoria Basham, Ngoc Du Thai Thi, Debbie Licorish, Jindy Pettman, Dan Brook, Senam Anderlini, Ghazal Zulfiqar, Ann Smith, Vanessa Farr, Dyan Mazurana, Isabel Geuskens, Lory Manning, Wenona Giles, Sandra Whitworth, Erin Leach, Ray Acheson, David Vine, Jana Lipman, Catherine Lutz, Kathy Ferguson, and Bob Benewick.

Yes, there are a lot of people to whom I am grateful. But it takes a lot of people to keep one alert, to challenge one's too-easy assumptions, and to inform one about subtle new trends. They each, and all together, have taught me about how gendered militarization works its ways into our lives. Each person here also has reminded me of what it means to stay intellectually curious and politically engaged in such a militarized world.

The Japanese feminist researchers of Ochanomizu University's Institute for Gender Studies, who planted the seeds for the Tokyo lecture series and then oversaw the publication of the resultant Japanese book, deserve special thanks: Professors Kaoru Tachi and Ruri Ito and all the splendid feminists on the staffs of the institute and its publishing house. They introduced me to other Japanese feminists who were carefully tracking militarism, its gendered causes and consequences: Suzuyo Takazato, Fumika Sato, Yumiko Mikanagi, Hisako Motoyma, Kozue Akibayashi, and Mina Watanabi.

The thoughtfully provocative scholars who launched this innovative Rowman & Littlefield book series and continue to inspire new authors to contribute to it are Professors Terrell Carver and Manfred Steger. It was Terrell, himself a prominent interrogator of masculinities, who convinced me that one book in the series should tackle the interplay of militarization and globalization *and* that an explicitly feminist approach would make the book more valuable.

At Rowman & Littlefield, Jennifer Knerr was the editor who first saw the promise in this ambitious globalization publishing project. When she moved on to other exciting publishing ventures, the project was energetically picked up by Susan McEachern. Susan is the guiding force behind this new edition. Every book you read has been made more readable by the professional attention devoted to it by an editor.

I am fortunate indeed to be partners with Joni Seager, a worldly feminist geographer and environmentalist, for whom no place is too remote and no authority immune to challenge.

As they say, "It takes a village." For this book to reach your hands, it has taken a globalized feminist village.

Chapter 1

Words to Investigate By

Today's world is historically remarkable for its level of globalized militarism. That is, the world we now are living in stands out from eras that our parents, grandparents, and great grandparents lived in because of the number of state militaries that exist—almost 200—together with the multiplying numbers of illegal (though many are tolerated by some officials) armed militias and insurgent armies, plus the growing numbers of local and national police forces that are now militarized and the array of private security companies that have been launched.

This, however, is only the tip of the current militarization iceberg that characterizes today's world. Add to the militarizing brew the multiplication of companies (private and state-owned) that produce and sell weaponry, or earn profits from selling non-weaponry goods and services to state and private military forces. That combined list is long: defense manufacturers, advertising agencies, fast food companies, garment makers, engineering and scientific research laboratories, transport companies, landlords, pharmaceutical companies, computer software companies.

Then pour into this already potent mix the expanding reach of media that feature stories of patriotic warfare or military adventure and heroism. Add every father, mother, girlfriend, husband, or wife who currently takes pride in (or relies economically on) a soldier or militia fighter. And do not leave out voters. Every woman or man who casts their ballot (if they are not subject to intimidation) freely for a particular party or candidate on the basis of that party's or candidate's support for a stronger military or for militarized responses to current crises (e.g., the arrival of refugees or migrant workers) is doing their own part to fuel militarization.

These powerful and globalized processes of militarization are not rolling forward, however, without resistance. The level and diversity of that resistance is also a hallmark of today's world: the proliferation of local and transnational peace groups, the launch of university peace studies programs, the spread of non-compliance movements in countries that still have compulsory military service, the multiplication and growing diversity of Nobel Peace Prize recipients, the growing numbers of electoral candidates who run on platforms of reducing military budgets and demilitarizing police forces, the increasing attention of many agencies of the United Nations to preventing and ending armed conflict. These mark our current era too.

To make sense of this militarized world—to support it knowingly or to effectively critique and possibly challenge it—requires that one become equipped with relevant, reliable ideas and the skills that one can put to work in one's own investigations. Some of the most valuable ideas take the form of concepts.

Concepts are tools. They should be useful. Every concept's worth is measured by what it reveals. If any concept that is offered hides more than it reveals, or distorts more than it clarifies, it is not a useful concept.

If a concept is well-honed and tested against messy realities and then refined, it can become a tool that enables us to craft reliable explanations of how this world works.

To investigate the gendered dynamics behind the globalization of militaristic ideas and practices, observers have fashioned particular concepts. These are widely used by investigators today because they have shed light on patterns that otherwise have been left in the shadows. Take, for example, the concept of "femininities."

Femininities: These are the variety of ways to imagine how girls and women think or behave—or *should* think and behave. Those imaginings comprise ideas about femininity. The workings of status-based, ethnicity-based, race-based, or class-based stereotypes serve to diversify these gendered standards and expectations of femininity. Thus, for instance, the woman who is the employer of a domestic worker and the woman whom she employs might each be pressured to be "feminine," yet the two women are expected to express their femininities in quite different ways, usually because of widespread class presumptions mixed with racialized and ethnic presumptions about how a particular sort of women should think and behave.

Any particular notion of femininity can be wielded by those people intent upon socializing, training, controlling, and even rewarding a girl or a woman for certain sorts of behavior: "Girls don't play that game!" or "A respectable woman doesn't go there!" or "You're such a good girl to help your mother with the laundry!"

However, any given package of ideas about what constitutes "real" femininity has been the subject of challenge. Tracking femininities in any community at any time requires being on the lookout for blatant and subtle forms of resistance: for instance, which girls insist on playing sports with the boys? Which woman speaks out at a public meeting, despite the misogynist ridicule hurled at her?

The transgender movement of the current era has built upon this understanding of femininities as unrealistically and unfairly confining.

Feminist analysts are especially wary of the concept of femininities precisely because those ideas—and the enforcement of those ideas—have served to sustain oppressive systems of power and today remain so restrictively potent in diverse women's lives. In many contemporary societies, to be conventionally feminine is to take satisfaction in one's dependency, not pursue autonomy, be silently ashamed if sexually assaulted, and not insist on one's rights.

Historically, the most globalized target of protest against restrictive standards of femininity has been the formerly widespread presumption—held by many women, as well as most men—that it was unfeminine for a woman to cast a vote in her country's elections. Women's suffrage movement activists in countries as different as Britain, Brazil, and the Philippines were campaigning not just for the right to vote, but to overturn established ideas about femininity, especially the idea that to remain acceptably feminine a woman had to stick close to home and rely on her father or husband for opinions about public affairs (Seager 2009).

In the twenty-first century, perhaps the target of protest that has been the most globalized has been the presumption that husbands have the masculinized right to use violence against their wives *and* that a "feminine" wife will keep silent about that violence, imagining herself to be worthy of blame for her husband's assaults. The fact that "domestic violence" is a term now common in so many national and international policy-making forums is evidence that this long-held presumption is being effectively challenged, even if the gendered acts of violence themselves are still rampant.

To make full sense of how gender dynamics may shape the processes of globalization, one has to explore the workings not only of femininities, but also of masculinities. Today, it seems to take extraordinary political will to shine one's searchlight on masculinities because that requires questioning men not just in their roles as, say, bankers or policy makers or athletes or soldiers, but *as men*. Most public officials shy away from doing that.

Masculinities: These are the variety of gendered ideas about how boys and men should think and behave. Manliness, that is, is a package of ideas about how an authentic boy or a "real man" should engage with others and with the world at large. Masculinity, however, is not singular, because societal notions of allegedly genuine manliness so often vary according to presumptions about marital status, class, ethnicity, and race.

For instance, many people (women and men) may accept certain behaviors as manly when engaged in by rank-and-file male soldiers ("boys will be boys") that they would find shocking if engaged in by senior male officers. Likewise, colonial and neo-colonial relationships between men have been, and today still are, fraught with contested notions of manliness. Gay and transgender men have been among those who have most directly challenged common notions of what constitutes standards of masculinity.

Gender is neither static nor monolithic. It evolves over time. We have learned in recent decades to pay attention to gender when it drives a social change process, and not always a positive social change process.

Feminization: This is the process of enforcing the idea that any particular thing is "naturally" or "especially" aligned with women, girls, or the alleged qualities of femininity. Anything can be feminized: bank telling, kindergarten teaching, crying, caring for wounded male soldiers, being the vice president for human resources, sewing globalized sneakers.

In a patriarchal society, those people and activities that are imagined to be feminized are accorded lower status, less respect and influence, and lower pay than those that are imagined to be masculinized. In many countries, among the most commonly feminized roles are nursing, sewing clothes in a garment factory, assembling electronics in a computer assembly plant, elementary school teaching, doing paid domestic work, taking care (for low pay or no pay) of children or elderly people, doing secretarial work.

In a patriarchal society, some men may disparage or discredit their male rivals by trying to portray them as feminine.

Masculinization: This is the process of promoting anything as "naturally" or "especially" aligned with men, boys, or manliness. In countries that otherwise might seem quite dissimilar, many of the same roles have been masculinized: soldiering, playing professional contact sports, being a senior professor of the natural sciences, directing Hollywood movies, managing a factory, presiding as a senior judge, piloting jet planes, making exceptional profits as an entrepreneur, rising to a senior religious position, and crafting the state's national security strategies.

Anything that has been masculinized can be demasculinized. In a patriarchal organization or society, this demasculinizing process results in the role losing its former prestige, political influence, and compensation. For instance, in many governmental systems today, where once no women were appointed to the governing cabinet, now it is thought by male leaders that the ministries of environment and of education are "appropriate" for women to head precisely because political leaders do not take the work of those department seriously. A classic example that feminist historians have explored is bank telling. In the early era of banking, being a bank teller was deemed a thoroughly "manly" job. Today, in most industrialized societies, bank telling has lost its prestige and thus now is occupied largely by women. Thus the processes of masculinization and of feminization both need to be watched carefully, society-by-society, over time. As feminist analysts remind us, those processes usually determine who can wield power and who can become the objects of that power.

With these four concepts—femininities, masculinities, feminization, and masculinization—in one's tool kit, one is ready to try one's hand at a gender analysis. It won't be easy.

Gender analysis: To analyze anything is to take apart its several elements in order to explain why it is the way it is. Thus to analyze the 2016 American presidential election campaign—or the 2015 election campaigns of, say, Turkey, Canada, or Myanmar—the analyst will have to consider all of that campaign's relevant players (candidates, donors, media, voters) and how their relationships to each other created the political outcome it did. Similarly, to analyze the multiyear war in Syria, the analyst will need to sort out all of the players and how the dynamics of their relationships escalated the violence endured by Syrian civilians, while they simultaneously made it excruciatingly difficult to end the violence and create some semblance of peace. To analyze anything—your family, a police department, the treatment of refugees, the fashion industry, global warming—requires the analyst to carefully watch it over time, and to figure out what are its crucial elements in order to determine both causes and consequences.

To conduct serious gender analysis involves monitoring and recording women's and men's, boys' and girls' ideas about and practices of masculinities and femininities. The gender analyst keeps a sharp eye out for any processes—successful or failed—of feminization or masculinization. The gender analyst, however, recognizes that femininities and masculinities are both multiple and fluid and that, therefore, living as a woman or being a man can take myriad, often unconventional forms. Yet working as a gender analyst, one is aware that under many circumstances there are pressures exerted by particular players to enforce certain standards of masculinity and femininity, and thereby to make gender practices unrealistically rigid.

Moreover, the gender analyst is always curious about how the workings of ideas and practices of race and racism, of ethnicity and ethnocentrism, as well as of class and classism, each operate in a particular time and place either to enforce or to dilute, maybe even subvert, ideas and practices of masculinities and femininities. A gender analyst, consequently, is always on guard against treating all men or all women as homogeneous—in their ideas, actions or their experiences.

Such a lazy homogenizing assumption is certain to produce unreliable analyses.

To analyze any war, any election, any policy process, any family, any industry, or any institution, the gender analyst always starts by asking, "Where are the women?" and "Which women especially are there?" The gender analyst follows up by asking, "Where are the men?" "Which men especially?" The gender analyst continues by asking, "Who did what to place those women here and those men there?" and "Who benefits from those men being there and these women here?" as well as, "Who is most disadvantaged by this gendered arrangement?" The gender analyst then tries to find the answers to the questions, "What do these women think about being here, and what do those men think about being there?" "How do they cope?" and "When do they resist?"

That is, the gender analyst cannot just be a watcher; being a trustworthy gender analyst requires that one also become an attentive listener. The gender analyst is keenly interested in those who seem to have little influence, as well as those who wield notable power. It is only by revealing the gendered relationships between those with and those without power that one can yield valuable explanations.

The gender analyst, furthermore, cannot afford to have a short attention span. One always has to ask these hard questions over time. Gender analysis is not very useful if it is just a snapshot at one moment in time, since that is likely to hide both gendered root causes and longer term gendered consequences. Start early. Stick around.

As one becomes a more skilled gender analyst, one will find oneself becoming wary when commentators casually refer to such ungendered categories as "mining executives," "climate change deniers," "cabinet ministers," "peacekeeping troops," "garment workers," "militia fighters," "SUV drivers," "children," "foreign policy elites," "domestic workers," "weapons manufacturers," "refugees," or "peace agreement negotiators." One will never know how much the particular gender dynamics shaping any of these groups influence their attitudes and behavior until one draws back the curtain and explicitly investigates those gender dynamics within each of these deceptive categories.

Becoming a consciously *feminist* gender analyst entails becoming committed to uncovering the power implications of every gendered dynamic, every gendered transformation. One certainly can conduct nonfeminist gender analysis, but it isn't very useful if one hopes one's analysis will become a foundation for creating effective change.

Only when one has developed gender analytical skills will one be able to determine whether—and why—one's society, school, workplace, political party, or social movement operates as a patriarchy. Patriarchies come in many guises, but they all marginalize women and empower certain sorts of masculinity. Being able to tell if any community or organization is patriarchal is necessary for tracking the causes and consequences of both localized and globalized militarism.

Patriarchy: As varied as patriarchal communities and organizations are in today's world, they share a common trait: each is a distinctive system of unequal relationships sustained by particular beliefs and attitudes which, all together, privilege certain forms of masculinity over all forms of femininity, even if some women are "placed on a pedestal" to be admired. Any society, organization, movement, or family becomes patriarchal when members adopt these femininity-disparaging, masculinity-privileging sorts of relationships, practices, beliefs, and attitudes. Patriarchy is not "old fashioned"; it is remarkably adaptable. It is constantly being updated, modernized by those who most benefit from it. Some patriarchies can even look "hip." For instance, the senior ranks of many Silicon Valley high-tech firms are notoriously masculinized. This is why patriarchies have proved so sustainable.

Patriarchal relationships often are reinforced by the workings of racism and class inequality, though patriarchy can be entrenched even in the most homogeneous of groups, the poorest of families, the most marginalized of communities. That is, no community is automatically immunized against becoming patriarchal. Black feminist analysts and anticolonial feminist analysts have insisted that, in trying to understand the lives of both women and men, the interplay of gender, class, race, and ethnicity have to be explored simultaneously.

Movements and institutions that promote capitalism and militarism are those which might appear to be the most likely to adopt—even cherish—patriarchal ideas and practices. Nonetheless, even those promoting antimilitarism, national liberation, and workers' rights can become deeply patriarchal when their leaders stubbornly embrace certain ideas about the superiority of particular forms of manliness and about the irrelevance of abusive behavior toward women. Being aware of this possibility has inspired women's rights advocates to carefully scrutinize seemingly progressive movements and organizations. It is just such scrutiny that weakens patriarchy's sustainability.

Now we can turn to concepts that are routinely investigated without much gender curiosity. Let's start with one of today's most widely used concepts, an idea employed for making visible a multistranded process of social transformation: globalization.

Globalization: This is the complex process—often taking decades, occasionally happening within a few years—by which any practice, any idea, any thing becomes widespread, across geographic regions and state boundaries. Croissants have been globalized, so have "action movies," sushi, the Kalashnikov rifle, women's suffrage, drones, Tweeting, cosmetic surgery, and camouflage casual clothes.

Today globalization is often thought to be fueled chiefly by capitalist profit-seeking. But other forces, such as consumer tastes, gender stereotypes and gender anxieties, homophobic and xenophobic fears, and antiterrorism nightmares and laws each also can be globalized through electronic social media, interstate alliances, as well as ideological and religious proselytizing. The desire for profits certainly matters, but, by itself, it does not explain enough about how and why particular globalizing processes operate the way they do today. Trying to make reliable sense of what propels globalization—and what forces resist it or slow it down—without asking gender questions and conducting gender analysis is likely to be futile.

A principal theme in discussions of globalization—its benefits, costs, and consequences—has been the mobility of manufacturing enterprises from country to country. The widespread analytical conclusion has been that company executives are always in search of cheap labor and that many national governments' officials are more than eager to offer up their own societies' cheap labor to the highest bidder. "Cheap labor," however, is a problematic concept. Thus it must be examined for not only what it reveals, but what it hides.

Cheap labor: No labor is inherently "cheap." It is *made* cheap—by someone. Workers' labor is *made* lowly paid or expendable by someone—usually a number of people in coordination—taking specific actions. Usually, it is employers who most directly take action to cheapen some of their employees' labor. Most often, though, employers need the cooperation of government officials to cheapen their employees' labor. These officials encourage employers to suppress workers' wages or look the other way when employers take these actions. They may do this out of an eagerness for state revenues or out of their fears of workers' independent organizing, or in exchange for bribes. Consumers are complicit in cheapening workers' labor insofar as they remain uncurious about the conditions under which the products they purchase are produced. Among the most common actions taken by employers to cheapen workers' labor are:

- wielding gender, ethnic, and racial stereotyping (usually in combination), including presuming that, allegedly because of their ethnic or racial backgrounds, certain workers are "naturally" good at only certain low-paid jobs and aren't worthy of training or promotion, as well as assuming that women workers will only work for pay until they are married or, even if working after marriage, are not "heads of households" and thus are earning merely "supplemental income."
- engaging in oppressive employment practices, such as compulsory overtime, unrealistic production quotas, sexual harassment, punitive pay cuts, unsafe working conditions, and hiring thugs to beat up any employees who voice dissent.
- devaluing certain skills, treating them as "natural" to those workers and thus not worth rewarding.
- prohibiting or coopting women's and men's workplace organizing to prevent those organizations from acting independently for workers' best interests.
- refusing to recognize women's and men's national and international labor rights.

Therefore, "cheap labor" is a concept of very questionable value. It hides more than it reveals. A far more useful concept, a concept that feminists now use to critique globalized political economies, is "cheapened labor" or "labor *made* cheap."

The present era has been marked not only by the processes of globalization and by the cheapening of labor, but also by the outbreaks of violent armed conflicts from Ukraine and Syria, to Congo, Palestine, Iraq, Yemen, Libya, Egypt, Nigeria, and South Sudan. It has also been an era in which it has proved extraordinarily difficult to create lasting peace in countries as different as Colombia, Mexico, Guatemala, Mali, Somalia, Myanmar, Northern Ireland, and Bosnia. Simultaneously, the manufacture and global trade in weaponry continues to burgeon, and many governments that are not officially "at war" find it, nonetheless, attractive to increase their military spending. As a result, many more people are drawing on the concept of militarism to help explain this three-pronged twenty-first century phenomenon.

Militarism: This is not simply a single idea. Rather, it is a concept that refers to a complex package of ideas that, all together, foster military values in both military and civilian affairs. Taken together, the package that is militarism also justifies military priorities and military influences in cultural, economic, and political affairs.

Among the ideas that go into the militarism package are:

- the belief that men are natural protectors and that women should be grateful for manly protection;
- the belief that soldiers deserve special praise for their contributions to their countries;
- the belief that hierarchies of command are a natural part of society;
- the belief that in human affairs it is natural to have enemies;
- the valuing of physical force over other modes of human interaction to resolve differences;
- the idea that any country without a state military is not a fully "mature" state.

There is plenty of evidence to demonstrate that not everyone thinks militarism is natural or valuable. For instance, the citizens of Iceland and Costa Rica have decided that their countries do not need militaries. Therefore, in order to investigate how it is that only some individuals, some groups, and some countries seem to adopt this distinctive package of ideas, while others do not, observers have crafted a second, complementary concept, militarization

Militarization: This is the step-by-step social, political, and psychological process by which any person, any group, or any society absorbs the ideas and resultant practices of militarism. Women and men each can become militarized, though usually they are militarized in rather different ways because militaristic ideas are so deeply imbued with gendered assumptions and values. Among those things that can become militarized are: a school's history lessons; the role of the "good wife"; a father's aspirations for his son; a government's annual budget; a national holiday's rituals; a voter's electoral choice; a civilian company's profit-making strategy; a town's sense of pride.

Militarization typically requires specific decisions to be made. Thus militarization is not inevitable. Reversing a militarizing process, however, almost always requires serious rethinking of ideas about femininity and manliness.

Demilitarization: This too is a step-by-step process. Demilitarizing anything entails making it less dependent than it has been on militarized values or on the military's approval for its worth, its influence, or its sense of well-being. Among the many things that can be *de*-militarized are: national security, political candidacies, school curricula, a marriage, the meaning of patriotism, standards of masculinity, a country's standing in world affairs, and a corporation's profits.

In today's world, one of the hardest concepts to untether from its militarized anchor has been national security. Women and men determined to advance demilitarization, locally and globally, thus have had to take a hard look at alternative notions of national security and at those who seem to have the biggest stake in keeping the concept of national security deeply militarized.

National security: This is the alleged goal of state officials when they devise policies to provide their citizens with protection from potential harm. In practice, national security's articulators—legislators, civil servants, intelligence agents, cabinet officers, judges, academic advisors, media commentators—often prioritize less the security of the diverse nation—the collectivity of civilian residents—and more the narrower interests of the state.

Security does not have to be militarized. National security could be measured by how many of its citizens have access to adequate nutritious food and decent shelter. Alternatively, national security could be measured by how much trust the poorest members of the society have in public officials and their institutions.

When national security as a concept is militarized, threats appear magnified, enemies seem to multiply, secrecy is more easily justified, intrusions of the state into civilians' lives are easier to rationalize, and compromises to civil rights can become legitimized. Moreover, when national security becomes militarized, the space where national security policy making takes place becomes a particularly masculinized arena of state affairs, an arena in which anyone imagined to be feminine does not seem to belong.

No concept is sacred. No concept should be chiseled in stone. Any concept worth its salt is vibrant, always subject to reassessment and fresh understandings. To be reliable, therefore, any concept needs to be constantly applied, tested, evaluated, and refined. The next gender-curious investigator may offer refinements that will make that concept more useful to all of us.

Chapter 2

"Feminist Curiosity" and Globalized Militarism

Developing a "curiosity" involves exploring, questioning—refusing to take something for granted. One is not curious about the things one takes for granted. For instance, most of us most of the time (unless we have a rotten cold or have started going to yoga classes) aren't very curious about breathing. Too many of us most of the time don't spend much time wondering about the extended droughts and melting arctic ice caps.

A major theme we will chart here is "feminist curiosity": How to develop it? What's distinctive about it? We will discover what it is that a feminist curiosity can reveal about the workings of globalization and militarization—and the links between them—that we would otherwise miss. In other words, this is a very practical, down-to-earth enterprise.

Developing a new kind of curiosity is not just academic. It takes energy. It is political. It is cultural. It is personal. To insist upon posing questions about things that other people take for granted can be a political act.

A feminist curiosity is a crucial tool to use today in making sense of the links between two of the world's most potent trends: globalization and militarization.

Like any "ization" (e.g., industrialization, urbanization), both globalization and militarization are actually many-layered processes of transformation. For instance, it turns out to be possible to track, step by step, strategic decision by strategic decision, precisely how the Nazi regime of 1930s Germany transformed the conscience of so many ordinary Germans. Advertising techniques and popular moviemaking played central roles (Koonz 2003). Thus you will need to watch trends in globalization and militarization over time and you will need to keep your eye on several layers at once: observing individuals change at the same time as you are paying attention to changes occurring in local communities, public institutions, companies, and whole societies. It's a tall order. Using a feminist curiosity should help all of us do it more realistically and with more reliable results.

Globalization is the step-by-step process by which anything—a movie industry, vegetable production, law enforcement, banking, the nursing profession, higher education, an individual's own sense of identity, human rights, environmental activism, or a women's movement—becomes more interdependent and coordinated across national borders. Nurses—usually women—migrate from the Philippines to hospitals in New York; Hollywood producers make films with few words and a lot of masculinized action so they can draw movie-going crowds in China; Chilean farmers produce blueberries that are consumed in the depths of winter in Toronto; Canadian mining executives, mostly men, anticipate a peace agreement in Colombia so they can expand their mining operations in this war-torn country.

Or think about the globalization of rubber. The first time I wondered where the rubber for my car's tires came from was when I was a graduate student living for a year in Malaysia trying to understand the ethnic tensions inside this former British colony's complex education system. My little apartment, though, was in a new development just outside the capital on land carved out of a rubber plantation. So in addition to education politics, I began to ponder rubber. There were rubber trees just outside my back door. In the early morning I watched rubber tappers working, skillfully slicing crescent-shaped cuts into the dappled bark of the slender rubber trees, then placing underneath the new cuts small cups into which the rubber tree's treasure, white liquid latex, would drip. Standing there in the early morning tropical light, I thought about the tires on my VW Beetle. But I don't think I realized that I was watching globalization at work.

For it was British scientists a century ago who surreptitiously took rubber trees from Brazil to their famous Kew botanical gardens in England, developed a commercial strain of rubber trees, transplanted them in their then British-ruled colony of Malaya in Southeast Asia, and hired thousands of Indian migrant workers to tap the white fluid latex flowing from the slim rubber trees on their vast plantations. The result: Dunlop, a British company operating rubber plantations in Malaya, became an international powerhouse when the development of the auto industry made rubber tires essential to modern transportation world-wide. The American company Firestone similarly used Liberia and France's Michelin used Vietnam to develop their global tire and rubber businesses. And other iconic American companies such as Singer, maker of the famous Singer sewing machines, were consciously developing global marketing strategies by the early twentieth century (Domosh 2006). So globalizing trends—in science, political control, labor migration, product marketing—are not new. What is new is the scale and breadth of globalizing trends since the late twentieth century, accelerating into the current century.

Often *globalization* is used as a shorthand label only for the worldwide sprawl of capitalist business organizations and flows of technology, labor, and capital designed to enhance the profits of those businesses. Likewise, then, *antiglobalization* is used to refer to the many-stranded social movement inspired by critiques of that capitalist globalizing trend. But it is more useful to understand that globalization can happen to anything, not just to profit-seeking companies and their products and employees. In fact, the antiglobalization movement, with its loose but often effective networks of environmental activists, antisweatshop activists, prodemocracy advocates, and local culture defenders, is itself a major result of globalizing trends: activists in Nigeria are now trading information and strategic lessons with people in Canada, Britain, and India.

On the other hand, it is true that not everyone enters into globalization with equal resources: not everyone can afford jet travel; not everyone has easy access to the Internet; not everyone has scientific laboratories or banking credit at their fingertips; not everyone has equal access to English, the increasingly dominant "lingua franca" of globalized communication; not everyone gets to discuss their international issues privately over cocktails with a senator.

Militarization may be a less familiar concept. But it too is a transforming process that happens over time—sometimes rapidly, though often at a slow, hard-to-spot creep. And like the process of globalization, militarizing trends can simultaneously change the influence one person has on another, can alter how stories are interpreted, can turn meanings upside down. To become militarized is to adopt militaristic values (e.g., a belief in hierarchy, obedience, and the use of force) and priorities as one's own, to see military solutions as particularly effective, to see the world as a dangerous place best approached with militaristic attitudes. These changes may take generations to occur, or they may happen suddenly as the response to a particular trauma. Most of the people in the world who are militarized are not themselves in uniform. Most militarized people are civilians.

A husband's and wife's marriage can become militarized if the husband decides to enlist in his country's military and that military operates on the assumption that a soldier's spouse will put the needs of the soldier in the family ahead of any other marital need. If a wife finishes her engineering degree and decides to accept a job offer to work for a large corporation that relies on defense contracts from governments and expects its engineers to accept a culture of secrecy, that can create deep pockets of silence within the couple's now-militarized home life. Similarly, a town's elected officials can become militarized if they begin to think that getting and keeping a military base sited nearby enhances the town's economic health, or if they believe a local weapons-producing corporation offers the best chance for sustaining decently paid jobs for their residents. Hundreds of towns around the world today are militarized (Vine 2015).

A government's international intelligence service can be militarized if intelligence gathering is done chiefly by the country's department of defense. Even if an independent intelligence agency exists on the government's organizational chart, intelligence gathering and, especially important, the interpreting of that intelligence, can become militarized if in daily reality it is the defense bureaucracy that possesses the greater budget and resources to conduct its own intelligence operations—and the country's elected representatives accept this as normal or even effective.

A country's international borders likewise can become militarized if a majority of voters and their representatives begin to think that danger lurks on the other side of those borders, dangers that must be addressed not through cultural understanding, diplomatic negotiations, immigration regulations, and ordinary policing, but instead through fortification, militarized policing, and even the deployment of soldiers. Such border transformations can spark intense public discussions and debates over whether militarization is the most useful process by which to address the movement of peoples from state to state in today's increasingly globalized world.

Border police and intelligence agencies are two of the most likely engines of militarization in today's world. The less that border police and intelligence agencies are held effectively accountable by democratically elected civilian authorities, the more prone that country will be to further militarization. In countries as different as Italy, France, and the United States, police forces have been equipped with military-scale armored vehicles and weaponry. This sort of equipment sends out a double message: to police officers, the message is: "Your fellow citizens are the enemy." To the civilian residents of towns policed by officers militarily equipped, the message is: "Your local police see you as threats, not as fellow citizens." Such a double message is doubly militarizing.

A civilian court judge can become militarized if that judge begins to believe that she or he must defer to a government lawyer's claims that, when a government agency is sued by a civilian plaintiff, the government's need to protect "national security" trumps all other claims before the court. Judicial deference in the face of executive branch claims of national security necessity is one of the most common modes of judges' militarization. That is, militarization can look less like conventional aggressiveness and more like deferential passivity.

Ordinary citizens can become militarized whenever they start to think that the world is so dangerous that the necessarily slow processes of legislative hearings, compromise, and open voting don't match the sense of speed and urgency—and maybe secrecy—they have come to think are needed to address those alleged dangers. This is the point at which officials in the executive wing of government—presidents, prime ministers, politically appointed officials, career civil servants—may think they have been given the green light to act behind the legislature's back, without public oversight, in the name of protecting the public from the perceived danger. If some members of the elected legislature also share this sense of danger and urgency and the resultant impatience with compromise and transparency, then that green light will shine all the more brightly. An elected legislator becomes militarized when she or he starts to demote civil liberties to second place among public priorities behind purported military necessity. Any civilian voter assessing the legislators becomes militarized when she or he begins to see military solutions to international problems as more effective than the often painfully slow and complex diplomatic solutions.

A globalizing corporation becomes militarized insofar as its executives come to believe that its overseas factories will be more secure if the foreign government is willing to use military troops or militarized police to put down labor protests.

This book explores how these two potent contemporary trends—globalization and militarization—often feed each other. For example, globalized militarization occurs when a foreign-owned corporation chooses to locate its contractors' factories in a country whose government is quick to wield military force against employees who call for better working conditions. *Globalization can become militarized.* Globalization depends on militarization whenever militarized ideas about national security come to be seen as central to creating or sustaining certain international relationships.

Similarly, *militarization can be globalized.* Think of all the national and international sales of rifles, land mines, armored vehicles, submarines, fighter aircraft, uniforms, body armor, radar systems, guided missiles, drones, and unmanned surveillance aircraft. There are so many players involved in the design, manufacture, sale and purchase of these militarized products—scientists, engineers, assembly line workers, executives, lobbyists, secretaries, accountants, marketers, middlemen, buyers, and users—that peace advocates, just to track the complex flows of large and small arms, together worth billions of dollars, have formed several independent, globally conscious groups: for instance, the Small Arms Survey, based in Geneva, Switzerland (www.smallarms survey.org); the Stockholm International Peace Research Institute (SIPRI) (www.sipri.org).

Just looking at the contracts won by the largest military defense corporations from the U.S. Department of Defense in fiscal year 2014, one finds Lockheed Martin at the top of the list, winning 8.84 percent of all Defense Department contracts, worth a total of $25 billion. Next in line is Boeing, followed by General Dynamics, Raytheon, and Northrop Grumman. Each of these corporations shapes the lives of thousands of employees—and those family members and local communities that depend on their wages. Number seven on the list caught some observers' eyes: It was not American. The British company BAE Systems was the only non-U.S. company in the "top ten" for 2014 (Aeroweb 2014). It had benefited from the "special relationship" between the U.S. and British governments in foreign policy, which persuaded Pentagon officials that, while not American, BAE could be trusted with contracts for sensitive weaponry. BAE's executives said it was not really an anomaly but an indicator of more to come—namely, defense manufacturers headquartered in diverse countries seeking profitable weapons contracts from any government eager to buy (Wayne 2006).

While it is usually the large companies producing the large weapons systems that make the news, small weapons kill more people day in and day out around the world. Where do the guns and ammunition that are causing death and dislocation among thousands of civilians in the Darfur region of Sudan come from? How do they get from their manufacturers to Sudan? Who is profiting?

Consider the recent emergence of globally active private security contractors, such as Blackwater USA (in the wake of a scandal, its owners renamed it Xe Service). Unlike the more familiar defense manufacturers, private security contractors actually provide, for substantial fees, the services formerly provided by governments' own militaries and police forces—guarding embassies and mines, providing food for soldiers, running supply convoys. Most of the recruits working for American, British, Fijian, and South African private security contractors are men (Eichler 2015). By 2006, in Iraq alone, in the midst of that U.S.-led war, nearly 50,000 private military and security personnel had been contracted by the U.S. government, private businesses (including newspapers and television companies), and the fledgling Iraqi government to provide various services (Holmquist 2005; Koppel 2006).

In addition, there are scores of companies—some little known to the public, others as well known as Halliburton, AT&T, Pizza Hut, Pepsi,

McDonald's, and Burger King—that may not deliver armed men overseas, but do make profits by providing goods and services to soldiers in war zones and on military bases. Many civilian military spouses have found low-paid jobs at these fast food restaurants, though in 2014 several of these companies decided to close some of their military base outlets rather than meet the Department of Labor's new minimum wage rules (Jowers, 2014).

Or imagine a map of the world showing all the military bases—large and small—that just the U.S. government operates. Today, there are an estimated 800 overseas American military bases. U.S. military bases currently stretch from Cuba, South Korea, Australia, and Britain to San Diego and Pearl Harbor, from Qatar and Bahrain to North Carolina, Washington State, and Arizona, from Colombia, Djibouti, and Egypt to Kenya and Uganda, from Japan, Poland, and Hungary to Aruba, Kwajalein Atoll, and Guam. In Germany alone today there are 134 American bases, in Japan 113, in South Korea 83, and in Italy 50 (Vine 2015, pp. 4–7).

These bases and their immediate neighborhoods take the mundane forms of barbed wire, tarmac, playgrounds, bowling alleys, bars, discos, grocery stores, medical clinics, tattoo parlors, tailors, mechanics shops, target ranges, fuel tanks, file cabinets, memos, emails, Facebook friends, love letters, sexually transmitted diseases, local civilian employees, spouses, children, private contractors, takeoffs, landings, parades, and pornographic DVDs. Together, however, these everyday base fixtures, personnel, and operations, as well as the typically secret official negotiations that create and sustain this worldwide network of bases, have produced a globalized process of militarization.

On every domestic and overseas military base, the daily relationships inside the wire are gendered. The relationships between the people working inside and those living in the local communities surrounding each base are also gendered. The dynamics of masculinization and feminization do not respect the physical boundaries (Enloe 2014; Gillem 2007; Hirshberg 2012; Lutz 2002; Vine 2015).

Again, some of these globalizing militarization engines were fired up more than a century ago. The imperial governments of Britain, France, the Netherlands, Spain, Portugal, the United States, and Belgium deliberately exported their own models of militaries to the countries they colonized around the world. Britain sought to replicate the British army in India, Nigeria, Malaysia, Fiji, Australia, and Egypt, complete with its own homegrown presumptions about ethnic hierarchies and notions of "martial races"—that is, ethnic groups whose men were imagined by the colonizers to be "traditional warriors" (Barkawi 2006). Britain's imperial rivals did the same in Indonesia, Vietnam, Mozambique, the Philippines, Senegal, Algeria, Peru, and Mexico (Enloe 1980). Recently, the British military is seeking recruits into its own military from young men in its former colonies, especially Fiji and Nepal (for its famed Gurkha regiments) (Gillan 2005; Ware 2012). When you next hear about Gurkhas serving in private security companies or in the British or Indian or Brunei armed forces on peacekeeping or disaster relief missions around the world, think of the long-lasting gendered militarized legacies of imperialism, as well as the hopes of young men and their parents in impoverished former colonies (Chisholm 2014).

So the globalization of militarizing processes is not new. What is new is (a) the global reach of these business, cultural, and military ideas and processes; (b) the capacity of promoters of globalizing militarism to wield lethal power; (c) the fact that so many private civilian companies are now involved in this globalization of militarization; and (d) the intricacy of the international alliances among the players.

Asking feminist questions is a valuable means of understanding how and why both the globalization of militarization and the militarization of globalization happen. Posing feminist questions, furthermore, can help reveal the potential consequences of these processes for both women and men. Each of us probably has had the experience—with friends, with family, perhaps even with teachers—of insisting upon asking about things that others would much rather take for granted. They think you are a nuisance to be posing these questions:

> "Dad, how come on farms producing food for export it's usually the women who do the weeding?"
> "Well, because they always have. That's just the way it is! Anyway, what's the big deal about weeding?"

Of course, we might be the lazy ones. Other people might have to nudge us toward becoming curious. Perhaps we are the ones who don't want to be bothered asking new questions. It can be quite comfortable taking a lot of things for granted. That is why it takes so much effort by so many people to turn something most people take for granted—the fact that it is mainly women who weed, the fact that miners breathe in coal dust, the fact that many high school students join a military cadet corps, the fact that people become poorer as they grow older—into an issue.

Something becomes an "issue" only when a lot of people do two things: first, they start questioning it and stop taking it for granted, and second, they begin to believe it deserves public attention and public resolution. Persuading people to do both of these things is not easy. Since so many cultures and so many governments treat women's experiences as not worth exploring and create the impression that the condition of women is merely a private matter, converting any aspect of women's lives into an issue has taken—and still takes—enormous effort.

For instance, if a lot of people begin to be curious about why it is mainly women who weed, but they still stop short of calling for public responsibility for this situation, then the fact that it is mainly women who weed won't become an issue. However, even the emergence of just a popular curiosity about why women are designated as the weeders may, further down the road, provoke people to call for more public responsibility for the causes and consequences of that agricultural division of labor. They may start looking into the international politics of cotton, of strawberries, of coffee.

Creating a new curiosity is an important first step—and it's not so easy to take. But nothing can become an issue if the exercise of curiosity remains a private activity or if what you uncover is deemed unworthy of public response.

So it is tough to turn something into an issue. Issue making is a political activity. It requires developing a new curiosity plus spreading that curiosity among a lot of people in their roles as public citizens. Think of all the things that today are being treated nationally or internationally as issues, things that fifteen years ago were not considered "issues." When, for example, did male soldiers' use of women as prostitutes become an issue at least in a few countries? How about "stalking"? When did militaries' use of land mines become an issue? Becoming an issue is never automatic. Each issue's development has its own history. Each issue needs to be explained. Every issue has become an issue only because some people stopped taking it for granted, developed a new curiosity about it, and managed to persuade a lot of us who used to be complacent about it to become newly curious, too—and to start finding answers that made them think afresh about citizens' and governments' responsibilities for those dynamics that they had discovered.

Developing a feminist curiosity can be energizing. It motivates one to treat as puzzling the relationships of women to any aspect of social life and nature that other people take for granted. So many people in most societies usually say (and many of us said before we began to cultivate our own feminist curiosity) that we do not need to ask about the condition of women or assumptions about women because they are "natural" or because they are "trivial."

"Mom, why do all these carmakers drape women models over their new automobiles?"

"Oh, dear, don't worry. Nobody takes that seriously."

Beware the adjective "natural." Beware "trivial." Both are boulders rolled up against a door you may want to open. Rolling away those boulders can take a lot of intellectual and social stamina. Using a feminist curiosity, one discovers that who weeds is not "natural"; it flows from who is assigned to weed, which child is pulled out of school because a life of weeding won't require the ability to read and write. Who is assigned to weed may determine who in the village is not trained to operate a tractor. Who weeds may turn out to have a lot to do with who is not legally permitted to inherit land. Following the bread crumbs of these questions reveals that "Who weeds and who doesn't?" is not a trivial question to pursue. It is a question whose exploration can shed a bright light on globalized agriculture, on who benefits from it, and on who stays mired in poverty because of it.

Developing and using a feminist curiosity does take a lot of energy. Many of you might have sat in a class and felt hesitant to raise your hand to ask a question, sensing people around you letting out an audible sigh, "Oh, there she goes again." It takes energy to go ahead and ask that question, to not let a misleading assumption about women or about men, about boys or about girls just slide by. Continuing to pose feminist questions even takes a kind of courage.

"Thinking about your lecture about international terrorism, Professor, shouldn't we ask 'Where are the women?'"

Or: "Excuse me, but in your discussion about nuclear proliferation policy, do you think that it matters to ask about international contests over masculinity?"

Exercising a feminist curiosity, therefore, is not a passive endeavor. It is not a quiet intellectual pastime. It is intellectual, but it takes stamina. Exercising a feminist curiosity calls on us to develop a kind of politics that has to be nurtured and cultivated; it does not just grow by itself. There will be those listeners who will raise their eyebrows skeptically or theatrically roll their eyes when a friend or colleague poses a feminist question. Each raise of an eyebrow, each rolling of eyes should be recognized as a political act. Each of those gestures is meant to discredit, maybe even to silence, the feminist questioner. Each of those gestures is meant to keep the boulders firmly up against the patriarchal door. Thus each gesture is worth investigating.

This book also calls on us to move beyond an interest in the impacts of global affairs on women—though those impacts are important and do need careful monitoring. This book is a call to action, a call to use a feminist curiosity to develop explanations—that is, to discover causes.

"Move beyond impacts to causes." It sounds deceptively bland. Yet wielding a feminist curiosity, one finds that one is not just spelling out the impacts (consequences) of anything on women, but delving into whether pressuring women to act and believe in certain ways actually explains why something has occurred: the outbreaks and perpetuation of wars; the spread of certain industries from rich countries to poor countries; the continued abuse of the environment (yes, it could be that it will take a feminist curiosity to fully explain why those arctic ice caps are melting).

Explanation—the discovery of what causes what—is the "brass ring" of any analytical endeavor. If you can discover a cause for something, you are on your way to creating a theory about it. A theory is an explanation that is backed by specific publicly shared evidence. Moreover, an explanation does not rise to the status of a theory until it has been reliably tested.

Still, let's look for a moment at impact analysis. It requires curiosity, too. And getting a feminist curiosity onto the agenda when people at the table are choosing what questions will be asked about impacts—outcomes, consequences—can be a challenge. Ask anyone with a feminist curiosity who has worked for a corporation, a local government, an international agency, a humanitarian aid organization. "What will the U.S. government policy of requiring the teaching of sexual abstinence in order to qualify for reproductive health aid mean for girls' relationships to men in Uganda?" "What did sending thousands of male UN peace-keeping forces into East Timor mean for those Southeast Asian women?" Getting their colleagues to take seriously the weighing of the impacts on women of any action the group is about to take can be a frustrating endeavor.

Often, even if official pronouncements are made calling for the condition of women and the ideas of women to be taken seriously, the actual institutional response is merely a token response—that is, officials go through the superficial motions, but don't alter their masculinist practices and policy presumptions (e.g., they appoint a "gender advisor" to their department but starve that person of resources and leave that person out of the loop of crucial information flows needed to do the job effectively). This has happened in national militaries, corporate businesses, and international agencies. Thus, developing the finely honed skills to distinguish tokenism from genuine change is useful when dissecting both globalization and militarization.

A "gender impact analysis" is a new tool in local and global policymaking. Gender impact analysis should be—but is rarely—completed before any final decision is made; decisions such as allowing a new foreign company to come into one's region or country to open a new copper mine, signing an alliance with another government that entails building a new air force base, permitting a foreign film distribution company to buy up most of the country's movie theaters, and legalizing a new anti-AIDS drug call for asking:

- How will this decision (in contrast to the other options on the table) affect men? Which men especially?
- How will this affect women? Will it affect certain women more than other women?
- How will this policy choice affect the relationships between women and men? Will it shrink the inequalities? Widen the disparities? Globally or locally or both?

Gender impact analyses are difficult to do. It takes skills and training. Some professional schools are still refusing to incorporate this training into their curriculum, depriving their students of the skills they will need. Today, however, those gender-analysis skills are being taught in new graduate programs and special training programs all over the world. Networks of feminist scholars, women engaged in local women's groups, and feminist-informed agency staff members are meeting, for instance, in Canada, Colombia, Thailand, and Kenya to write new gender-analysis training manuals and to create new courses to increase the number of people who have the skills to perform gender investigations and assessments of policy proposals. These gatherings don't make headlines, CNN and Reuters crews don't arrive there with their cameras. Nevertheless, the women and men who travel across time zones to take part in these meetings are helping to globalize a feminist curiosity. Among today's most effective globalized feminist networks are:

- Women Living Under Muslim Laws (WLUML), whose activists, themselves women from Muslim backgrounds, monitor and challenge nationalist discourses, religious intolerance, sexist laws, and sexist practices rationalized in the name of Islam and nationalism. Its activists publish a newsletter from Pakistan and organize international solidarity campaigns to support local women subjected to patriarchal Islamist regimes (www.wluml.org).
- Women's International League for Peace and Freedom (WILPF), celebrated its 100th anniversary with a large meeting in The Hague in April 2015. It was founded in The Hague in 1915, during World War I, by 1,300 women activists from Europe and North America who opposed that devastating war (one million men were killed or maimed in the stalemated muddy trench warfare in France in the five-month Battle of the Somme alone) and now has its headquarters in Geneva, with active branches in Colombia, Sweden, Norway, Burundi, Ghana, Sierra Leone, Canada, Russia, Japan, Australia, the United States, and twenty other countries (www.wilpf.org; www.peacewomen.org).
- Women's Initiatives for Gender Justice, based in The Hague, is a newer network of feminists who organized to monitor and pressure the new International Criminal Court (established in 1999 as the first international war crimes court). Its members take actions to ensure that systematic rape and sexual slavery in wartime are explicitly recognized and prosecuted as war crimes (www.4gender justice.org).
- Women Waging Peace, first launched by a former U.S. ambassador who had seen firsthand the impact of war on women in Bosnia during the early 1990s, as well as local women's own courage and

organizing skills, has become a network designed to support and build bridges between often isolated local women's peace groups, among them groups in the Congo, Bosnia, Georgia, and Sierra Leone (www.womenwagingpeace.net).

- Women Peacemakers Program, based in the Netherlands, works with affiliates in Burundi, Sudan, and other countries whose women and men are coping with the violence and legacies of war. It also works with the Dutch government to ensure that UN Security Council Resolution 1325 on Women, Peace and Security is fully implemented (www.womenpeacemakersprogram.org).

- Women in Black, a network of women in countries around the world—in Israel, Serbia, Spain, Italy, Japan, the United States, Britain—who oppose militarism and its roots in patriarchy and nationalism and who hold silent vigils open to all women, standing prominently every week in their own city's busy intersections (Cockburn 2012; Women in Black 2005).

Two WILPF leaders have been awarded Nobel Peace Prizes (Jane Addams in 1931 and Emily Greene Balch in 1946). Women in Black's Belgrade and Jerusalem groups were nominated for the Nobel Peace Prize in the late 1990s.

All six of these globalizing feminist networks have made the exposing of, and the rolling back of, local and international militarist policies, ideas, and practices central to their work. Members of all six global networks also have become convinced that, given the ways in which hydra-headed militarization works, the most effective actions are those that not only are sensitive to local cultures, politics, and priorities but also embrace international alliances in which to share ideas and information and to coordinate actions. Members of all six of these groups, furthermore, have become convinced that women have special roles to play in exposing and challenging militarization, not because women are somehow innately, biologically wired for peacefulness, but because women are so often outside the inner circles where militarizing decisions are being made yet are likely to be called upon to support, and even work on behalf of, militarizing agendas.

That is, members of all six groups, while they differ in their ways of organizing, their modes of resistance, and their country focuses, share a conviction that we must take women seriously and that it is crucial to challenge those particular ideas about masculinity, about femininity, and about patriarchal social orders that they have come to see as the local and global engines of militarization (Bauer and Helie 2006; Cockburn 2012; Cohn 2013; Confortini 2012; Giles, de Alwis, Klein, and Silva 2003; Hawkesworth 2006; Kaufman and Williams 2010; Sjoberg and Via 2010; Spees 2003; Stiehm 2006; Women in Black 2005; Women Waging Peace and International Alert 2005).

Yet many international and national decision makers prefer to switch off their curiosities and to leave these new feminist analytical tools to rust in the basement. If the policy elites did use the gender analysis tools, they might have to change their agendas. For example, if they commissioned gender impact analyses and then acted on their findings, officials in natural disaster relief agencies might have to significantly reallocate their resources. When planning for future tsunami, earthquake, or hurricane relief, many people (though not all, and not necessarily those with authority) have learned the hard way that it is always important to ask ahead of time about the likely impacts both on women and on men—of every economic class, of every ethnic group. Why? Because, of all the thousands of people who died in the giant waves set off by the December 2004 Indian Ocean tsunami, a majority turned out to be women and their dependent children. Likewise, in the chaotic aftermath of Hurricane Katrina, which devastated the Gulf Coast of the southern United States in September 2005, it was African American women and their dependent children who were especially endangered by the lack of government preparedness and the resultant overcrowding of unsanitary emergency shelters.

Look at another recent example of how a serious engagement with gender impact analysis would push officials to alter their political decisions. In 2005, the Iraqi and American male political elites who together hammered out Iraq's first post-Saddam constitution deliberately inserted (or passively allowed) provisions for putting much of family law—those laws determining marriage, divorce, child custody, and inheritance—under the influence of conservative male clerical officials. Some Iraqi women went into the streets in the summer of 2005 to protest. But these women's advocates weren't inside Baghdad's fortified, exclusive Green Zone where the U.S. administrators had their offices and where the constitutional deals and compromises were being made. These Iraqi women were certainly talking about gender impacts; they were convinced that inserting these conservative provisions into the new constitution would push most Iraqi women further out to the margins of the country's public life. But neither the American nor the Iraqi officials wielding the most influence in the constitutional process ordered a formal gender impact statement to be written or to be discussed in public or to be taken into serious account by senior negotiators. Iraqi women activists—and they grew in number as the war dragged on, despite the risks involved in being publicly visible as women as the violence escalated during 2005 and 2006—were shut out of high-level American and Iraqi elite policymaking. Iraqi women activists didn't lead any of the Iraqi political parties; they didn't control any U.S. or new Iraqi army or police regiments or the multiplying sectarian Iraqi militias; they didn't occupy the positions of clerics or of media editors. Those were the people being taken seriously, and they were virtually all male. The result: passage of a new constitution that many Iraqi women's rights advocates believed would undermine even the status women had under the former authoritarian regime (Al-Ali and Pratt 2009; Enloe 2010). Today, as the Syrian war has spread to Iraq, Iraqi women continue to contend with this patriarchal political system crafted by men waging the previous war.

Impacts matter. Wielding a feminist curiosity about impacts is a valuable analytical activity. When that feminist curiosity is not used, there are real-life consequences.

So, when we weigh whether we need to "go beyond impacts to causes," what is being considered is not that we should stop posing gender impact questions. In fact, many women's rights advocates have urged that compulsory "gender impact studies" be included in the negotiating process by which every piece of legislation and every international agreement is hammered out. No hurricane prevention or relief plan should be approved, no constitution should be ratified, no foreign investment should be okayed, no new military base agreement should be signed until there has been a thorough and public accounting of the potential impacts on women, on men, and on the relationships between women and men (equalizing or unequalizing). Yet when we "go beyond impacts to causes," we gain something more.

To make sense of today's complex world, we need to understand that many decisions have not only gendered consequences but also gendered causes—that is, causes flowing from presumptions or fears about femininity or masculinity. It is only by using our feminist curiosity that we can expose these gendered causes. For instance, certain phrases do not merely have a destructive impact on certain women; the popularity of those phrases is caused in part by ideas about women, by presumptions about femininity and masculinity. Creating a feminist causal analysis takes us to a deeper level of understanding of how and why the world "works" the way it does.

Thus, one of our newest feminist revelations is that one cannot explain why the international system works the way it does without taking women's lives seriously. "Experts" may be knowledgeable about banking interest rates, about the oil industry, about HIV/AIDS; nevertheless, if those experts fail to think seriously about women's lives, they are certain to produce a deeply flawed understanding—explanation—of today's international political economy. An example: there is a rising awareness that HIV/AIDS is being spread because of armed conflicts. The simple causal explanation thus might be that "war causes AIDS." But feminist investigators have found that that level of causal explanation is just not adequate. After all, firing a gun does not spread the virus. Rather, these investigators have found, it is the increasing sexual violence by men—men armed with weapons and with masculinized arrogance and often ethnic or racial contempt—against girls and women in the midst of armed conflict that is causing the spread of the deadly virus (Lewis 2005; Russella et al. 2015).

Saying that taking women's lives seriously is necessary for developing reliable explanations about much of what is going on in the world, including the interactions between militarizing change and globalizing change, is a radical feminist assertion. The term radical comes from the ancient word for root. So to say that this is a radical feminist assertion is to say that it is going to the root of how we understand militarized globalization or globalized militarization. It is an assertion that anybody who is interested in international politics—a legislator, a journalist, a professor, an activist, your boss, or your best friend—but refuses to take women's lives seriously is going to be an unreliable guide into today's and tomorrow's international system.

True, this is a risky assertion to make. You should not just swallow it. You can do your own evidence gathering, your own testing. Then, out of that exploring, you can reach your own thoughtful conclusions about the value of this feminist causal assertion about how globalization and militarization work.

CHAPTER 3

TRACKING THE MILITARIZED GLOBAL SNEAKER

Let's start testing this feminist causal explanatory tool by looking at the international politics of factory work. If we consciously use a feminist curiosity, we can see how the promoters of globalizing factory work maximize their profits by relying on manipulations of ideas about "femininity" and the "dutiful daughter" and then enforcing those manipulations with militarization.

That is, the efforts of companies and governments to make—and keep—their factory workers' labor cheapened often become dependent on militarism. The result: many of the sneakers—and shirts, jeans, as well as football, soccer, and basketball uniforms—that look white or red or blue or neon pink on the surface may turn out to be threaded with khaki on the inside.

"Cheap labor" is the work of some employees who are paid relatively little for their skill and effort. Our challenge: to question this commonly accepted (i.e., *un*questioned) notion of "cheap labor" by using a feminist curiosity. This won't be easy because "cheap labor" is a phrase so commonly used to explain the increasingly globalized world we live in:

"Oh, Company X is moving its factories to Asia because they're attracted by its cheap labor."

Or: "Sure, the Mexican government is going to win out over the Canadian government in attracting foreign investment because the Mexicans can offer companies cheap labor."

Women's labor is especially likely to be thought of as "cheap." Men's labor—particularly the labor of men from poor countries and ethnically and racially marginalized groups—also can be thought of as cheap. Think about the history of cotton, gold mining, and the building of railroads; think of Asian men trafficked to serve as slave labor today aboard fishing ships (Urbina 2015). In the past 150 years, however, industrializers have discovered "femininity." Thus it has been women's labor that has most often been imagined by economists, development planners, and factory owners as allegedly "cheap," that is, worthy only of low pay and minimal workplace safety.

In globally competitive industries such as the textile industry, the garment industry, the shoe industry, the processed food industry, the electronics industry, and the toy industry, therefore, it has been women who have been deliberately hired to produce goods cheaply. Look at a Barbie doll and ask about women's cheapened labor; consider computer chips and ask about women's cheapened labor; hold up a pair of blue jeans or a football uniform and ask about women's cheapened labor.

Staying uncurious while employing the easy phrase "cheap labor" depends on assuming that the labor of women inevitably, unavoidably is cheap. That lack of curiosity depends on making the deeper assumption that women's labor is "naturally" cheap, that women's labor is automatically cheap, that women's labor is cheap in a way that requires no policy decisions, no pressure, no manipulation. If we take for granted that women's labor is inevitably cheap labor, then we (students, civil servants, legislators, economists, activists, corporate executives) can comfortably move right ahead to build our corporate strategy or our international development plan without disturbing this unexplored assumption.

Alternatively, let's look at a radically different analytical possibility. Using a feminist curiosity, let's pose a question: Is women's labor *made* cheap? As soon as one starts using this new phrase—"women's labor made cheap"—one finds oneself motivated to ask another new question: by whom?

Your curiosity now is being energized. You are inspired to ask even deeper questions. Digging deeper, you start asking: How is any woman's labor made cheap?

Now you are on an analytical roll. There is no dampening your feminist curiosity. You have lots of new questions to pose about globalized (and also localized) women's factory work. Making—and keeping—women's labor "cheap" does not look so easy anymore. It looks as though it takes efforts by myriad actors. And so the international practice of using women's skills, talents, attentiveness, and energies begins to seem more political, more dependent on the wielding of power—psychological, cultural, legal, economic, and (as we will see) maybe even militarized power. Militarized police, for instance, are routinely called in by those employers who have nurtured close affiliations with government officials in order to quell labor demonstrations organized by women factory workers who have decided that their labor should not be "cheap." This is one way to militarize women factory workers' globalized labor.

Vietnam has become a favorite country for brand-name sneaker corporations and their factory contractors. The government is dominated by a single political party. There is very little room for organized dissent. Since 1986, though nominally a Communist Party in power, the Vietnamese political leadership has energetically pursued foreign capitalist investment in order to achieve its economic development goals. Young Vietnamese women were offered up as available and cheapened labor to foreign brand corporations and their factory contractors (mostly businessmen from Taiwan and South Korea). Many of the young women hired to sew and glue sneakers migrated from rural villages to Hanoi and to Ho Chi Minh City (formerly Saigon).

To assure those companies that they will have optimal operating conditions, Vietnamese officials have not permitted any independent labor union organizing. Simultaneously, the government's own regulatory agencies, responsible for enforcing labor rights and safe working conditions, have been deliberately under-staffed and under-funded.

According to the feminized stereotype, women workers are obedient, they don't organize, and they don't protest. In 2006–2007, that stereotype was proved wrong. Vietnamese women factory workers, producing shoes for Nike and Adidas, went on unauthorized strikes. They were protesting their low pay and their managers' insistence that they work long hours of overtime. Each time, the government put down the women's protests using military troops (Ballinger 2010).

Despite these protests, or because of the government's effective suppression of those protests, by 2014, more and more global sneaker and shoe manufacturers—Timberland, Puma, Nike, and Adidas—were shifting their orders from feminized factories in China to feminized factories in Vietnam. Chinese women sneaker workers were organizing unauthorized strikes that were resulting in their gaining somewhat higher wages (World Footwear 2014). Today, the globalized race continues: Which male-dominated government can entice the greatest number of male-run sneaker brand companies and their male factory contractors to their countries by using force to keep their local women's labor "cheap"? This is not simply a globalized capitalist race. It is a globalized patriarchal race.

Anything that is described as "natural," therefore, should be carefully examined under the feminist curiosity microscope. If it is labeled "natural," allegedly, it took no effort to make it that way: "Today thousands of women in factories all over Asia stitch Nike sneakers. So what? What is interesting about that? Women stitch. Women have always stitched. Sewing, it's just what women naturally do. They like it."

Ha!

A little aside here: I grew up outside of New York City, a classic American postwar suburban teenager. When I was in middle school, all girls were required to take home economics—cooking, sewing, and hygiene. Of course, the boys went to separate classes where they were taught carpentry and car repair. We girls were taught how to scramble eggs and sew a hem. What I learned back then, long before I became a feminist, was that sewing is not a natural skill for all girls or for all women. In fact, it was so unnatural that it took the help of three of my mother's friends to get me through the sewing section of that home economics course. I was failing, so my splendid mother, who also did not sew, had to phone three of her suburban friends to help little Cynthia get a skirt sewn that would pass muster. Therefore, when one sees a girl or a woman sewing, stitching at home or in a factory, one needs to explain how she learned that skill, who decided it was a skill she (not her brother) should learn, and why. If it's not "natural," then it needs to be explained. Calling for an explanation is a political act.

So the first assumption to investigate in any examination of women in globalized factory work is the assumption that the women in the factories are there because they are doing naturally what women always do. Who benefits from this widespread assumption? It will probably turn out to be an alliance of diverse beneficiaries: mothers, fathers, brothers, boyfriends, government planners, local factory managers, foreign corporate executives, overseas retailers, and shoppers looking for bargains.

This act of feminist curiosity will prompt one to be skeptical about three additional common assumptions that are made today by "experts" in international political economy: *first*, the assumption that no government official (in alliance with company executives) ever had to think about ways to put women there on that factory floor; *second*, the assumption that no government official (or company executive) ever had to think about how to keep women there; and, *third*, the assumption that no company executives ever had to sit around the table and devise strategies to create and sustain an alliance with local government officials for the sake of making (and keeping) women's pay low and their labor thereby "cheap." Three assumptions. These three assumptions amount to three failures of curiosity that create three dangerous analytical traps.

A nonfeminist investigator of globalized capitalism assumes that no corporate executives ever had to hold a serious business strategy session to figure out how to keep women's labor cheap. That same investigator of international capitalism also imagines—lazily—that no corporate manager ever had to strategize about how to work with local government officials in order to get the "kind" of women—or girls—they wanted: old or young? urban or rural? local or migrant? married or unmarried? ethnicity A or ethnicity B?

The analysts who make these lazy assumptions usually are not challenged by anyone. They are thus allowed—by their supervisors, by their clients, by us as consumers—to go on making these flawed assumptions about women who work in international trade. Unchallenged, they continue talking about "cheap labor." They continue to discuss globally competitive trade or export processing zones, as if their expert understanding of international politics were rational, complete, reliable, and realistic.

It is not.

In reality, this widely used approach to the politics of global business, with its lack of a feminist curiosity, is too simplistic. It is an approach that hides power. Once you adopt a questioning feminist curiosity, you begin to notice how many decisions, how many calculations, how many strategy changes it actually took to get those women into that factory. Suddenly you realize it took a lot more corporate and governmental thinking, the allocation of a lot more resources, and the wielding of a lot more power to get that woman to do (and to keep doing) the allegedly "natural" work she is doing—stitching a sneaker, assembling a microchip—for lower pay than the casual users of the phrase "cheap labor" have been willing to admit.

When I gave a talk in Tokyo several years ago, I asked everyone in the audience to take off their shoes and to look at the labels inside to see where their shoes were made. I deliberately wore my sneakers that night. Professor Chizuko Ueno, the evening's discussant, and Professor Yumiko Mikanagi, our moderator, two well-known Japanese feminist scholars, both joined our collective investigation. We began with Professor Ueno. She found that though she'd purchased her fashionable, shiny black Reebok sneakers in New York, they had been made in the Philippines. Professor Ueno exclaimed, "So, actually I have caved in to exploitation!"

I tried to reassure her: "You have a lot of company. That is why I wore my sneakers tonight. I thought that I could not talk about how women's pay is made so low and pretend that I am not taking part in it too." My sneakers that night were New Balance—made in China. Others in the audience, doing research on their own shoes, started calling out the countries listed on the labels inside their shoes: "Brazil." "China." "China." "China." "Thailand." "Thailand." "Brazil." "Argentina." "Germany." "Japan." "China." "Thailand." "Indonesia." "Indonesia." "Vietnam."

A good starting point is to ask in which of these countries have women been sewing these shoes with little right to create their own independent unions. Then we should continue to pose questions: In which of these countries do executives and government officials agree that using armed force to intimidate women labor organizers is necessary for company and national productivity? Next: In which of these countries are women persuaded that they don't deserve promotions because they will be quitting paid work once they get married and become unpaid housewives? Then, in which of these countries are women employees afraid to demand better working conditions (for instance, less forced overtime) because they believe their primary duty as good daughters is to keep sending money home to their impoverished rural parents?

Posing these questions—country-by-county, brand-by-brand—and trying to reliably answer each of them, then weaving together the findings—that is what it means to do a gender analysis of the globalized sneaker industry.

Here is another research report "from the field." While still in Tokyo, I started going into the brightly lit sneaker shops along Tokyo's busy Takeshita Street. Here are my informal research findings: Converse low-top sneakers—so popular today in Japan and the United States—now are being made by women in Indonesia. Converse was bought by Nike in 2003, though it still markets its sneaker styles as counterculture fashion statements. One can conduct one's own research by reading sneaker labels in shops—in Durham, San Diego, Bogota, Stockholm, Leeds, London, or Seoul.

Style is political. In today's highly competitive globalized sneaker industry, the more elaborate the stitching, the more incentive corporate executives have to make the stitchers' labor "cheap." For example, envision the popular, multicolored Converse low-tops. They are among the least fancy of sneakers. "Hip," yes, but not fancy in either their materials or their stitching. Compare those low-tops now with the sneakers favored by soccer or basketball stars and the shoppers who admire their style. The fancier the stitching, the more necessary it will be for a sneaker executive to keep the stitchers' wages low in order to keep profits high. The more pressure factory managers and their corporate clients feel to keep the wages they pay their female workers low, the more tempting it will be for those same managers and corporate clients to tolerate militarized intimidation of their workers. Highly styled, complexly stitched sneakers—those sneakers for export whose profits depend on keeping workers unorganized—are more likely to carry a militarized price tag.

It was largely because the low-tops were designed with so little stitching that Converse kept its low-top factories in the United States, primarily in North Carolina, until the late 1990s. Although, prior to the buy-out by Nike, Converse's Boston-based executives decided to produce these low-tops in the United States, where wages are generally higher and safety regulations are generally more demanding, they chose a state, North Carolina, whose local lawmakers have given local factory workers only limited rights to organize labor unions. Furthermore, Converse's own personnel officers seemed (we do not know this for sure because no one has yet done a gender and racial study of a Converse factory in the United States) to prefer African American women factory workers. These are women who, due to North Carolina's long-time racialized gender politics, had limited job opportunities and thus had been least able to protest their low wages.

My sneaker research along Tokyo's bustling Takeshita Street revealed that, in the early 2000s, Converse executives changed their gendered global strategy. They moved their low-top sneaker production from North Carolina to Indonesia. Why? Was it just a calculation of kilometers? Indonesia is closer to Japanese teenage shoppers than is North Carolina. Or did the women working in Converse's North Carolina factories start organizing? And what gendered sales pitch did the Converse executives back in the United States hear from Indonesia's male government officials? Which gendered message about Indonesian women did Converse strategists hear from rival sneaker makers already manufacturing in Indonesia that made the labor of Indonesian women seem so economically and politically appealing?

The corporate decision makers of New Balance, also headquartered in Boston, adopted a different though still feminized geographic strategy. Until the early 2000s, New Balance executives marketed their global brand as "made in the USA," hiring mainly new immigrant women living in the Boston area to stitch their sneakers. They seemed to think that consumers would view New Balance as a more socially responsible company if they kept producing their sneakers in a country and a region that allowed its mainly female workforce to unionize. This practice also allowed the mail-order retailer L.L.Bean to feature New Balance sneakers in their popular catalogs with a good conscience. Although New Balance executives moved most of their manufacturing operations from Boston to China, Indonesia, and Vietnam, they sought to assure American consumers that New Balance still produces a higher proportion of its sneakers in the United States than does any other major sneaker company. One of the potential customers that New Balance executives have had their eyes on is the U.S. military. In 2010, New Balance opened a store inside the Pentagon. In 2015, executives even created a special model of New Balance sneaker produced entirely in the United States in hopes that, with it, they could win a lucrative contract for soldiers' training shoes from the Pentagon (Chesto 2015).

Dates matter. Historical development matters. Gendered uses of power, which push certain women to stitch and glue sneakers in certain countries more than in others, are not stagnant. A feminist curiosity is a historically lively curiosity. With a feminist curiosity, one keeps track of diverse women and ideas about diverse women around the world over time. The gendered global politics of sneakers—like all forms of gendered international politics—therefore has to be historicized.

Open your closet and look at all your shoes. Now line up all your sneakers according to the year in which you think they were made. Borrow your mother's and father's oldest pairs of sneakers, too, so that you will have a longer historical time line to work with. You will be prompted now to start asking feminist questions about the time-specific dynamics of women's labor, women's hopes, women's organizing, governments' competing industrial policies, and corporate executives' changing geographic calculations about how to make women's labor cheap. Which pair of sneakers is the most globalized? Which is the most feminized? Which is the most militarized?

The recent history of South Korean women working in sneaker factories makes this clear. According to investigations by women's studies researcher Seung-Kyung Kim, executives of American, European, and Japanese sneaker companies and electronics companies were deliberately wooed, starting in the 1960s, by South Korea's then-military government led by the authoritarian president Chung Hee Park, who was eager to achieve rapid industrialization and compete in the emerging global economy (1997). In crafting their strategy, General Park and his military and civilian economic advisors did not rely on the widespread flawed assumption that it was "natural" for Korean women to stitch sneakers or to assemble delicate electronics products.

These economic-policy strategists did, however, assume that women—especially young women—would be better stitchers than their Korean brothers. But they realized that sewing in their parents' homes and sewing in a Nike factory were very different ideologically.

Thus, in the 1960s and early 1970s, the military government of Chung Hee Park launched a calculated campaign to change Korean citizens' image of the "respectable" Korean young woman. Conflating the concepts of "national security," "national pride," "modernization," and "industrial growth," this military government set about to persuade the parents of daughters to radically alter their own definitions of what was "natural" for "decent" ("marriageable") South Korean young women to do outside their homes. The government's campaigners argued that a young unmarried woman who stitched, not under her parents' careful supervision, but instead under the supervision of a foreman in a factory miles away from home, could be endowed with a "respectable" femininity and an appealing feminized morality that would still make her attractive on the Korean marriage market.

Nike, Reebok, and Adidas could not be lured to South Korean factories in the 1960s and 1970s unless the Park military regime could transform Korean parents' ideas about what is "natural" and what is "respectable" behavior for "dutiful daughters." If we are not curious about mothers' and fathers' changed ideas of daughterhood, respectability, and marriageability, we will become unreliable analysts of the "Korean economic miracle."

Nike was the first sneaker company to shed its own factories and to start relying on subcontractors to own and to manage the factories producing Nike sneakers. Consequently, the Korean young women mobilized in the 1960s and 1970s to work as patriotic dutiful daughters in sneaker factories were not hired—or fired—directly by Nike. They were hired, disciplined, paid, and fired by the Korean male entrepreneurs with whom Nike signed contracts. The masculinized sneaker company executives from the United States and Europe were in part attracted by the fact that many of these factory-owning Korean men—subcontractors for Nike and later for Reebok and Adidas—enjoyed close political relationships with the militarized South Korean political elite. No matter what bright color sneakers had on the outside, by the 1970s sneakers were turning a distinctive shade of khaki underneath.

Threaded through virtually every sneaker you own is some relationship to masculinized militaries. Locating factories in South Korea was a good strategic decision in the eyes of those Oregon-headquartered male Nike executives because of the close alliance between male policymakers in Washington and Seoul. It was a relationship—unequal but intimate—based on their shared anticommunism, their shared commitment to waging the Cold War, and their shared participation in an ambitious international military alliance.

Pusan, a major Korean port and industrial city, became, by the late 1970s, the "sneaker capital of the world." By then, other sneaker companies had copied the Nike model. Here are the key elements of this globalizing industrial model that made Pusan so central to the world's sneaker industry: (1) close the company's own factories; (2) put the women employees who make the sneakers at arm's length by hiring local male subcontractors to run the factories and to make cozy alliances with the local male political elites; (3) view shared anticommunist ideologies as good for profitable manufacturing; (4) take comfort in a Cold War military alliance, as imagined by the U.S.-based company executives between "your" government and "their" government; (5) design corporate strategies to exploit local sexist ideas about femininity in order to justify low wages paid to young women workers; (6) depend on the local regime to craft a national ideology of "feminine respectability" that will enable your subcontractors to have a seemingly endless line of willing and unorganized women workers; (7) encourage consumers—women and men—in Japan, the United States, and Europe to imagine that they are "empowered" when they purchase and wear your high-priced sneakers; and (8) persuade these same consumers not to be curious about whether the Asian women stitching their sneakers also feel "empowered" when they go to work in Pusan's modern factories.

Any investigator of global political economy (or "development") who lacks a feminist curiosity will not even see half of the building blocks it has taken to create and sustain this popular formula.

This potent international formula was crafted in the 1960s and 1970s and continued to "work" for South Korean and U.S. and European policymakers into the mid-1980s. Despite significant changes in South Korea's political culture, especially the rise of a lively civil society, many elements of this gendered—militarized—neoliberal industrial formula still operates today. To tell whether—and why—any elements of this global sneaker industry formula have genuinely changed requires curiosity about the politics (local, national, and international) of both femininity and masculinity. Here is just a sampling of some feminist questions we need to find the answers to:

- To what extent do Nike's American male executives and their Korean (or Indonesian or Chinese or Vietnamese) male factory managers (subcontractors) use their shared masculinity to build trust between each other in what is a highly stressful global economic climate?
- Do today's Indonesian, Vietnamese, and Chinese women sneaker workers all have identical ideas about being "feminine" or being "dutiful daughters"?
- Do Chinese, Korean, Vietnamese, and Indonesian government officials promote the same feminized idea about the "model woman worker"?

In the early 1980s, a prodemocracy movement gathered steam in South Korea. Its chief goal was to force the twenty-year-old military-centered regime to turn over power to a popularly elected civilian government. At the outset of the movement, students at prestigious Korean universities provided the ideas, leadership, and members. But soon women and men working in factories began to take part. Participation in any prodemocracy movement is gendered—the risks taken, the nature of the consciousness change, the sorts of political influence gained and the goals set by the movement, as well as the rewards, are likely to be different for (and thus differently weighed by) women and men. Again, feminist researcher Seung-Kyung Kim (1997) provides us with insights into these often-ignored gendered realities of a prodemocracy movement's evolution. Many thousands of South Korean women working in sneaker, electronics, and garment factories in the early to mid-1980s began to imagine something new: that when they were working in these factories, they were acting as citizens. They began to believe that they—as low-paid factory workers—were not just "dutiful daughters," they were not just future wives; they were citizens.

How do companies and governments keep any woman's labor "cheap"? Policymakers encourage that woman to imagine that she is not a citizen when she is in the factory working those long hours, stitching Nikes and Reeboks on the assembly line, but, rather, she is first and foremost a dutiful daughter. Dutiful daughters obey supervisors; dutiful daughters think first of their parents' needs (and of their brothers' needs) and, second, about saving money for a future husband.

Therefore, if enough women on the sneaker assembly line begin to imagine that, as they stitch Nike sneakers, they are doing it not as dutiful daughters but as full citizens—that is, individuals invested with rights—policymakers in corporate and government offices are going to have a harder time keeping the labor of women "cheap." In European and North American countries, as well as in Asian, Middle Eastern, Latin American, and African countries, whole political cultures and legal systems have been cultivated over generations to discourage women from thinking of themselves as citizens. The reason it took decades of women's gutsy organizing to simply win the right to vote was that the men who ran governments, schools, newspapers, and churches stubbornly clutched onto the masculinist idea that the proper place for women was in the home, imagining them first and foremost as wives, daughters, or mothers, not as citizens (even if, in reality, many women were working in fields, in textile and garment factories, and in the kitchens and laundry rooms of wealthier people's homes). So the claim that they were citizens when they were sewing high-priced sneakers for export, not just daughters or would-be wives, was not a claim unique to Korean women workers. It was a claim that had to be developed and asserted by women in most countries.

Despite the risks, many South Korean women workers—though not all—did develop a new consciousness during the upheavals of the mid-1980s. It was this change in factory women's sense of who they were that then enabled a student-led prodemocracy movement to burst out of its own narrow middle-class confines and make alliances with working-class women and men.

We cannot just note this transformation that was to alter the global politics of the sneaker industry and then move on. We need to explain it. And that can be accomplished only by using a feminist curiosity. Without posing serious feminist questions, we will fail to adequately explain the success of the historic South Korean prodemocracy movement of the 1980s. Furthermore, if we don't look closely at the hopes, dreams, skills, fears, and strategies of these Korean women working in sneaker (and electronics and garment) factories, we will fail to see the causal connections between the ouster of the Seoul generals and the departure of Nike from Pusan. We will fail to see that individual women's rethinking of "respectable femininity," and "daughterhood" and their reimagining of themselves as "citizens" not only can bring down state regimes but can alter the calculus on which contemporary international political economies rely. A citizen-worker is no longer an easily cheapened worker. One might try to picture conversations in Nike's Oregon headquarters in the mid-1980s as so many South Korean women struggled to see themselves as citizens: "Get out the map, Bob, we're packing up in Pusan. Where is Jakarta?"

There was an opportunity in the late 1980s for the sneaker industry to remain globalized and feminized (reliant on women's assembly work) but become less militarized. If Nike and the other international sneaker companies had decided that the ouster of the generals and the success of the prodemocracy movement was "good for business" and thus had stayed in Pusan, the sneaker industry would have remained global—headquarters in one country, factory managers and assembly workers in another country, and customers buying their products around the world—but it would have adapted to South Korea's new significantly demilitarized political culture and relationships (including the newly energized labor movement and the increasingly vibrant women's movement).

But that was not the decision made by the sneaker executives head-quartered in the United States and Europe. They had gotten used to the business advantages offered by a militarized regime. If South Korea was going to roll back its own militarization even somewhat (not completely, as many Korean antimilitarist analysts are quick to point out), then the sneaker companies would move to another country where militarized politics were still entrenched. Indonesia looked appealing.

Capitalism (local and global) is not just about modernity. The architects of late-twentieth- and early-twenty-first-century capitalism have deliberately decided to exploit a false notion of tradition. In practice, this has proved a very tricky game to play. It takes clever footwork by state and company strategists to promote a capitalist brand of modernity by entrenching traditional daughterhood and traditional wifehood in the factory system. Stop. Reread the previous sentence. Slow down when you get to "by." "By" is the strategic "trick" here. One might think this "by" is easy to accomplish, that it is quite simple to entrench traditional ideas and practices of daughterhood and wife-hood—or one might imagine that these overseas-investing capitalists are just in a muddle.

Not so. Patriarchy routinely tries to hide its confusion. One of the tasks of researchers is to pull back the curtain of alleged coherence and rationality to reveal the confusion operating just behind it.

How that modernizing patriarchal capitalist confusion—evidenced by contradictions, mixed messages, ambivalence—is superficially rationalized and disguised is a question for any analyst who seeks to make sense of the contemporary international political economy. Thus we need to investigate both government officials' and company executives' mixed messages about daughters and marriage and simultaneously pay careful attention to girls' and women's own efforts to untangle and use these mixed messages. We have to craft the feminist curiosity and feminist skills to do both, because it is the dynamic intertwining of the two that helps shape what the globalized sneaker industry is today and what it is soon to become. We dare not be satisfied with a single still photograph. And we dare not let our attention wander.

In the late 1980s a major migration of an entire industry occurred. In search of the next population of "dutiful daughter" employees (in the name of industrial modernity)—and of a regime that would use its own authority to promote a revised "traditional" ideology of dutiful daughterhood—Nike, Reebok, Adidas, and other sneaker companies moved to Indonesia. They brought their Korean male factory-owning subcontractors with them, too. Indonesia's president was then General Suharto, head of a "New Order" militarized regime. Like General Chung Hee Park of South Korea twenty years earlier, General Suharto and his Indonesian male civilian economists, in pursuit of rapid industrialization fueled by foreign investment, set about to modernize the Indonesian idea of a respectable, dutiful daughter, though perhaps the Suharto officials took less initiative, instead following the lead of the foreign investors and their factory managers, who had their own clear ideas of what was "men's work" and what was "women's work" (Caraway 2007). Once again, with the aid of the popular media, mothers and fathers were convinced that letting a daughter move away from home to work in a sneaker (or electronics or garment) factory would not compromise their daughter's respectability or jeopardize her chances for a decent marriage.

By 2000, Nike and other global sneaker companies had (working with their Indonesian, Taiwanese, and Korean male subcontractors) hired 100,000 Indonesian women employees to produce their sneakers.

The Indonesians' pro-democracy movement of the late 1990s had pushed the country's generals out of power. Still, the years of military and militarized police having helped to keep thousands of young women from organizing, and thereby keep their labor "cheap," had consequences that have been hard to reverse. Today, the Indonesian women's movement is vibrant, union organizing is legal, labor advocacy groups have become politically significant, and women factory workers have been taking direct action to improve their working conditions.

Nonetheless, in the midst of these dynamic cultural, political, and economic forces, still entrenched is a myth about "traditional Indonesian femininity," routinely reinforced by local media narratives. These shape young women's own dreams of achieving a "good marriage," as well as their daily individual strategies for sustaining their reputations as a "respectable woman" under patriarchal scrutiny. All of these pressures, even in a society rightly proud of its democratic reforms, serve to keep Indonesian sneaker workers' labor "cheap."

When any government calls in security forces to put down labor protests by women sneaker workers (protests for decent wages, for the right to organize, for the end of forced overtime, for the end of sexual harassment by male supervisors), there is a gendered politics going on—on all sides. It is not just the women workers who are gendered. The men in the police and army units who confront them with shields, batons, and guns are also gendered insofar as they see their wielding of instruments of intimidation as expressions of their own manliness. In other words, whenever women workers are confronted by male security forces, we are witnessing feminized labor being deliberately intimidated with masculinized force. We need to direct our feminist curiosities both to the women working in the factories and to the uniformed men ordered by the government to keep them in line. At present, we know startlingly little about how these security forces and how these women experience—and strategize about—these sharply gendered confrontations at the sneaker factory gates.

So now, as the major sneaker companies—and their subcontractors—open scores of factories in Vietnam, Thailand, and China, we need to apply the same feminist curiosity to understand the extent to which current practices differ from the "model" created in Korea and the extent to which they are still the same. We need to make lists of what has changed and what has persisted. Neither Vietnam nor China has an overtly military regime in power, though each is governed by an authoritarian one-party regime. Until mid-2006, Thailand had a multiparty civilian government, but it was taken over by the military acting, it said, to end the rule of a corrupt and authoritarian civilian-elected administration. All three countries have strong masculinized police and military forces that are deployed against their own citizens in the name of public order and national security. All three of these governments, while religiously diverse, are male-dominated. And all three governments have attracted foreign investors by offering to mobilize millions of young women from rural villages to work miles away from home in new export factories. Is it pure oppression and intimidation that is making women's labor "cheap" in Vietnam, Thailand, and China, as well as in Indonesia? Or is it official intimidation and corporate profit strategizing combined with the government's manipulation of, and women's own evolving ideas about, femininity and marriage (Ballinger 2010)?

Before one imagines that there is no alternative to this widely entrenched system for making and keeping women sneaker workers' labor "cheap," it is worth looking at a small but imaginative experiment: a private company called No Sweat. The company lasted only four years. It ultimately was defeated in part by the difficulty in finding U.S. athletic clothing chain stores willing to carry a brand that explicitly challenged their stores' own principal corporate sponsors. That is, retail store chain executives, with their fears of upsetting their chief brand suppliers, should be added to the list of players who globally cheapen women's factory labor.

Yet No Sweat provides lessons about what an alternative to Nike, Adidas, Under Armour, and Puma might look like if executives weaned themselves—and their consumers—off an addiction to feminized "cheap labor."

In 2006, the company's website spelled out the owners' philosophy concerning globalization:

> We believe that the only viable response to globalization is a global labor movement. No Sweat defines the market for goods that support independent trade unions—the only historically proven solution to sweatshops.

Printed inside each No Sweat sneaker was the company's motto: "100% union made."

The company was co-founded in 2004 by Jeff Ballinger, an American labor rights consultant and monitor, together with three other partners. For years, Ballinger had been charting the practices of the sneaker industry, especially the use of factories in Indonesia. During the 1990s, while the Suharto regime was still in power, Ballinger regularly published a four-page newsletter exposing the labor practices used in Indonesian sneaker factories to keep women's labor "cheap." He called his modest publication "Nike in Indonesia." Gradually, this slim newsletter made its way into the hands of American op-ed journalists and even Gary Trudeau, the politically minded cartoonist whose "Doonesbury" strip appears in newspapers across the United States. Nike executives began to feel pressure from consumers. Even some of their highly paid sports-star endorsers, such as Michael Jordan, became defensive when asked why they were supporting exploitive labor practices.

Then came the 1998 prodemocracy movement in Indonesia, which toppled the Suharto regime. The political system opened up enough to permit some local labor unions to become more assertive on behalf of workers and to stop functioning merely as passive instruments of the government.

It was in this new, less-militarized political climate that Ballinger and his partners decided to launch No Sweat. They stayed in Indonesia. They were committed to proving that it was possible to create non-exploitation-reliant sneakers in Indonesia. They used their familiarity with the country's shoe business and relied on help from Indonesian labor advocates to compare factories. Were there any factories whose managers and owners were producing shoes without exploiting their workers? They finally decided on a factory owned by Bata, one of the world's biggest shoe manufacturers. They determined that Bata, which had a multigenerational history of paternalistic policies toward its employees, allowed their largely female workforce to join an autonomous labor union. That was No Sweat's core criterion. They also determined that Bata would provide workers stitching No Sweat's classic low-top black-and-white and red-and-white sneakers with decent, livable wages and employee benefits.

No Sweat inserted into each of its sneaker boxes a card to inform consumers of the pay and benefits its Indonesian workers received:

Hospitalization: Employee—100 percent coverage; Family—100 percent onsite, 80 percent offsite

Maternity (for female employee or wife of a male employee)—first child—225 rupees; second child—200 rupees; third child—150 rupees

Shift allowance: first and second shifts—175 rupees per hour; third shift (night shift)—200 rupees per hour

Working shoes (leather and canvas): two pairs per employee

Rice allowance: 30 liters per month

Ramadan bonus (most Indonesian employees are Muslim): eight weeks' salary

Pension: 3 percent contribution by the employee; 7 percent by the company

This does not mean that there is no room for exercising a feminist curiosity about this small innovative experiment in alternative sneaker globalization. Jeff Ballinger himself was candid about the limitations of the Bata/No Sweat labor union, SPSI, to which their employees belonged. In the past many of the male leaders of Indonesian labor unions had been more eager to protect male workers' benefits than to extend those of women workers, often seeing women workers as a threat to their male members' wages because they imagined factory managers were enamored with the strategy of substituting women for men in certain assembly line jobs where they could pay women less (Caraway 2007).

This perception of women workers as a threat to male workers' pay rates has been commonplace among all too many male union leaders in many countries, including the United States and Britain. Ballinger gave credit, however, to the activists inside the SPSI's Women's Bureau, an office created by women union members in the 1990s to focus especially on women workers' concerns and to monitor the union leaders' attentiveness to those concerns, especially regarding corruption and oppression and a decent national minimum wage. It was the combination of Bata's own particular corporate philosophy, the evolving democratizing culture in post-Suharto Indonesia, and the work of SPSI's women activists that made No Sweat's anti-cheap-labor global business experiment possible.

Neither globalization nor militarization is an inevitable process. Each can be stalled or even occasionally reversed. This is why using feminist curiosity takes stamina. One has to stay attentive.

Delving into the globalized and often-militarized evolution of the production politics of just one product, the sneaker, teaches us to direct our curiosities to more than simply business and government decision-makers. We need to expose how difficult it is to construct—and sustain—a kind of femininity that allows women's hard work to be cheapened, a kind of femininity that serves both corporate profit and a kind of masculinized state development strategy that depends on feminized cheapened labor. Crafting and deploying an energetic feminist curiosity will enable us to pose those questions that reveal the confusion hidden behind the patriarchy's facade of rationality, as well as the calculation and coercion that are required to get one woman to accept low wages and meager benefits in exchange for stitching one pair of globalized sneakers.

CHAPTER 4

HOW DOES "NATIONAL SECURITY" BECOME MILITARIZED?

Currently, among the most militarized regions in the world are Syria and its neighboring territories, as well as Colombia, the Kashmir-India-Pakistan region, the border regions of Russia, Afghanistan and its neighbors, the Persian Gulf, the border between North and South Korea, and the South China Sea. The myriad state officials—and their advisors and supporters—are the chief propellers of these geographically specific militarizations. To justify their militarizing actions, they usually talk in terms not of world security, but of the security of their own nations.

Because these regions have become so militarized, they also are regions in which social and political relationships have become extraordinarily masculinized. To note this does not mean that there are no women living in these regions. There are thousands of women living in each. What it means, instead, is that each of these rampant militarizing processes has had the effect of privileging certain sorts of manliness, each has marginalized other sorts of manliness (for instance, the masculinities attached to those war-fleeing men who have become refugees and of those men who have refused to join any of the state or insurgent militaries). Simultaneously, each of these militarizing processes today has downgraded or denigrated most forms of femininity, thereby marginalizing the majority of women. Women in these highly militarized, masculinized regions have gained visibility today only insofar as they are seen as silent victims or as compliant patriots.

Against all the gendered odds, in each of these eight currently highly militarized regions women's advocacy and support groups have organized. They have a hard time being heard: few journalists report on them; no officials ask for their advice. Instead, these activist women often are the targets of masculinized violence. Yet their presence—their advocacy and humanitarian efforts, their gender analyses—make the processes of localized and globalized masculinized militarism more visible.

Thus it is important to pay close attention, for instance, to women activists in Afghanistan, Russia, Ukraine, Bosnia, and Kashmir, and to women-led humanitarian aid groups inside of Syria and among Syrian refugees. Likewise, it is valuable for any gender analyst to pay close attention to those women transgressing the North and South Korean fortified border, and to those women who have created feminist peace activist groups in Colombia. Paying attention to their actions and their ideas enables us to see when and how gender dynamics cause each militarization and with what consequences—for both women and men (Butalia 2012; Humanas Corporacion Colombia 2013; Sperling 2015; Svedberg et al. 2013; www.humanas.cl; www.wilpf.org; www.womencrossdmz.org).

Many of the actions that serve to globalize militarization—that is, to spread the rationales and activities underpinning militarism—are, surprisingly, taken not in the name of *international* security but in the pursuit of *national* security. For instance, a government that calls upon its security forces to put down a workers' protest in an export factory might not claim that the workers' organizing is jeopardizing world peace, but that it is undermining the nation's security. Similarly, a country's government may join (or take the lead in creating) an international military alliance—taking part in joint military maneuvers, standardizing weaponry and procedures, buying each other's fighter aircraft, pledging to come to each other's defense, sharing intelligence surveillance reports—all in the name of enhancing its own national security. Nonetheless, the creation and operation of these policies serve to globalize militarism.

That is, national security and the globalization of militarization need to be considered together.

Following World War II, the study of national security became a common fixture in the curricula of many universities, military academies, and civilian schools of diplomacy around the world. "National security" was widely viewed as encompassing a government's military operations and alliances, as well as the underlying foreign policy doctrines and strategies—even if civilian officials were in charge of such matters.

Complementing this particular understanding of national security has been a widespread assumption about the sorts of people who make the most credible national security experts. It has been imagined that anyone wanting to be taken seriously in the field of national security—in government agencies, think tanks, graduate schools, on media news programs—has to be "rational." The opposite of rational has been imagined to be "emotional." Combined with this assumption is a common belief that "manly" men are the most rational beings, while less manly men and virtually all women are prone to being "emotional." This conventional gender package has made a certain kind of masculinity the entry ticket into national security discussions.

National security thinking (including taking part in often fierce debates among national security experts) has been portrayed as leaving no room for sentimentality: one has to be able to confront unpleasant facts "without blinking"; one has to be "hard nosed." Rational manly security experts must be capable of "muscular thinking"; they must never show themselves to be "soft."

Thus, in early 2015, when Sweden's new foreign minister, Margot Wallstrom, announced that Sweden would adopt a new, less militarized, approach to national security based on what she called a "feminist foreign policy," many national security commentators scoffed. How naïve! How unrealistic! And yet Wallstrom was anything but naïve. She had had more political experience than many of her critics. She already had served as a member of parliament for Sweden's Democratic Socialist Party and as a Brussels-based EU official and, most recently, as the UN Secretary General's Special Representative on Sexual

Violence in Conflict. In the latter role she was advised and supported by Swedish feminist groups such as Kvinna till Kvinna (Women to Women) (www.kvinnatillkvinna.se). As a government minister, she explained, her feminist foreign policy initiative stemmed from her conclusion that any country's genuine national security was guaranteed by crafting a foreign policy that pursued "peace, justice, human rights and human development." That combination of ambitious goals, furthermore, had the best chance for being reached if women were included in both analysis and decision-making. As she warned a Washington audience: "We won't get there without adjusting existing policies, down to their nuts and bolts, to correct the particular (and often invisible) discrimination, exclusion and violence still inflicted on the female half of us" (Rupert 2015).

How one thinks about national security, therefore, not only affects global relations but determines who is even allowed to sit at the table to take part in the security conversation. The more militarized the understanding of what national security is (and what it is not), the more likely it will be that the conversation about national security—and international security—will be a largely masculinized affair (Cohn, Ruddick, and Hill 2005; Sjoberg and Tickner 2011; Tickner 2001; Wibben 2011). Certainly, a handful of women might be allowed in now and then, but they will have to be constantly on their guard. They will have to make sure that they never appear (in the eyes of their colleagues) to be sentimental, emotional, or "soft"—that is, "feminine." And even many men will, under these restrictive conditions, have to be wary: if they betray emotion when they talk about the use of military force, they might risk forfeiting their masculine credentials, which in turn could mean their being shut out of future top-level discussions of national security.

Anything can be defined as a threat to national security, using the conventional understanding of that term, insofar as it appears to threaten the strength of the state. Thus, not just a foreign military mobilizing on the state's borders, but enemies far away believed to be planning to undermine the state by devious means may be viewed as threats to national security. Still other threats to national security can be seen close to home, posed by those inside the state. Most commonly, these people are labeled subversives. During the 1950s, in what today is looked back upon as the "McCarthy era," those Americans labeled "subversives" included Communists, Communist sympathizers (broadly defined), and homosexuals.

In postcolonial societies in the 1960s to 1990s, threats to national (state) security also included those women who were having "too many" children. The "population control" movement became a global movement, engaging scores of economists, demographers, development experts, and pharmaceutical companies (Hartmann 1995). Women were portrayed by each of these players as being a threat. Or rather, women's "fertility," if left uncontrolled, was deemed a threat—a threat to the country's economic stability and thus, allegedly, to the state's viability. Since instability in countries such as the Philippines, Kenya, India, Bangladesh, and China was viewed as exacerbating tensions in an already-fraught Cold War world, population control programs began to merge with militarized international calculations. Population control was a surprisingly masculinized global campaign (Hartmann 1995). Although men as sexual partners were left almost undiscussed and women of childbearing age were made the prime target of these programs, it was men who did most of the official worrying, scientific research, pharmaceutical promotions, and strategizing. While millions of dollars and thousands of person-hours were spent trying to control women's fertility—to get women to have fewer children—women themselves were hardly deemed national security authorities.

Then came "Cairo." It became a turning point in the security-focused international politics of population. Cairo, Egypt, was the site for the large UN-sponsored 1994 conference on population, which brought to that city experts and government officials from dozens of countries—some delegates from the countries posing a "population problem," other delegates from countries whose officials were committed to anti-abortion and anti-contraception policies, and still other delegates from the countries providing money to and directing population control projects in those other countries with the goal of enhancing their security.

But something had changed. Women's advocates—some calling themselves specialists in "women and development," others thinking of themselves as "women's reproductive rights" activists, still others openly taking on the label "feminist"—had learned the ways of the United Nations and the development bureaucracies of their own governments.

These women's advocates had seen what happened to poor women when they were mere objects of population-control projects. The advocates had developed international alliances and networks to push for women's health, women's political empowerment, and what many activists now called "women's environmental security," as well as women's economic independence, and most innovatively, women's sexual autonomy.

These women's activists who traveled to Cairo in 1994 succeeded in persuading the United Nations and the major governments orchestrating the meeting to call this conference not a conference on "population control," but instead, for the first time, the International Conference on Population and Development. In so doing, they forced a shift from a narrow, state-centered notion of security to a broader, more human-centered notion of security. Once the conference got underway in Cairo, these women from myriad countries—some rich, many poor—persuaded a majority of governments to publicly declare their understanding that anxieties about "population control" had to take a backseat to concerns for women's and girls' health and education.

Women hereafter had to be treated as actors in the development and security-creating policy and implementation process—actors with rights over their own bodies. Since the UN Cairo conference of 1994, certain administrations in some countries (notably those of the Vatican and of the United States in the early 2000s) have tried to undercut this Cairo global consensus. Nonetheless, after the Cairo conference, the international security discourse on population changed (Eager 2004). It could no longer be easily taken for granted that women's fertility could be reduced to a security issue for states, and more women concerned about the lives of women were actively engaged in the designing of health and economic, as well as environmental and foreign policy, research, and the crafting of the policies often flowing from this research.

In recent years, particularly just after the end of the Cold War, which brought with it the termination of the great-power rivalry between the United States and its allies on the one hand and the Soviet Union and its allies on the other (with many other less powerful countries left to carve out precarious spaces somewhere in the volatile middle between the behemoths), there was a flood of fresh thinking about security.

More questions are being posed these days about whose security should be prioritized. Some are asking what the difference is between "national" and "state" security. Is "human security" a more valuable way to conceptualize genuine security pursuits? People asking this question are suggesting that security is more likely to be realistically assessed and pursued if less emphasis is put on governments and their military capacities and more attention is paid to the needs that must be fulfilled for ordinary individuals to experience genuine security. For instance, maybe taking stronger action to stop global warming, to provide clean water worldwide, and to prevent the further spread of HIV/AIDS would move us closer to achieving meaningful global security than would investing so much energy and public money in developing fighter planes and recruiting millions of young people into state military forces (Basch 2005; Hoogensen and Stuvoy 2006).

This post–Cold War era was taking shape in the 1990s at the very same time that feminist scholarship investigating the complex workings of international affairs was beginning to make itself felt inside academia and international agencies. This development was the product of years of researching, teaching, and organizing. The reason that women are now considered important actors in measuring and pursuing alternative forms of less-militarized "security" is that this feminist work had been done.

So, as we now plunge into a discussion of national security—how it has been militarized and how it might be demilitarized—it is worth spending a bit of time here to look inside one academic organization where this development of alternative security thinking has gained prominence. Scholarly organizations—for example, the American Historical Association, the International Studies Association, the British International Studies Association, the Association for Asian Studies, the National Women's Studies Association, the American Political Science Association, the Modern Language Association, the Middle East Studies Association—may seem quite remote from the lives and studies of undergraduate students. But often, unbeknownst to students, these associations influence decisions about who earns a doctoral degree (and who is discouraged), what books and articles get published and assigned for courses, what sorts of topics are taken seriously in classrooms (and what topics get only minimal attention in a semester's syllabus), and what new interdisciplinary programs and majors are launched.

The International Studies Association is not one of the largest academic associations, yet it has been the principal forum in which both long-standing and new ideas about how to investigate and teach global affairs are compared and tested. While English remains the dominant language of the ISA sessions and its publications and many members of the ISA are American, many other members come from Sweden, Norway, Canada, Australia, Germany, Britain, India, and Japan. In a sense, the study of international affairs is itself becoming globalized. And while previously it was mainly political scientists and economists who came to ISA's annual meetings—as if it took only political science and economics to make sense of national security, international trade, war, peacemaking, migration, diplomacy, oil, and sneakers—today when the ISA gathers, the conference rooms, hotel corridors, and coffee shops are full of historians, sociologists, and anthropologists, too.

Simultaneously, and maybe as a result, the ISA—this transnational intellectual group whose members see themselves as the crafters of political skills and knowledge—has become far less masculinized. That is, there are more women taking part in its annual sessions and in running the organization, and it is less acceptable for men, who remain the majority of the organization's members, to dismiss the idea of women as experts and to devalue the study of women as "beside the point." This demasculinization—achieved slowly and through hard work—has made the association livelier, more open, more intellectually valuable.

The women—and a few men—who achieved this partial (but not yet complete) transformation of the ISA did so through several actions:

1. Back in the mid-1980s, these women began to urge other women whose work sheds light on any dimension of international relations to attend ISA's annual meetings.
2. Women faculty urged women graduate students both to attend the ISA and to propose their own paper presentations.
3. These women devised new conference panel topics in order to stretch ISA members' sense of what constitutes "international politics." For example, they created new sessions on "Trafficking in Women," "Gendered Humanitarian Aid," "Masculinity and Weaponry," "Feminist Theories of the State," and "Women in the Revolutions of Nicaragua, Eritrea, and Algeria."
4. They began to develop an alternative "culture" for their ISA panel sessions, making those events more interactive, more encouraging and less competitive, less hierarchical.

5. They created a new section within the association's organization, naming it "Feminist Theory and Gender."

6. A few years later, they launched a new ISA caucus specifically to monitor the relative influence of men and women on the ISA's governing committees.

7. More recently, the ISA's feminist-informed women and men created a new journal, the *International Feminist Journal of Politics*.

The twenty women and men who launched the *International Feminist Journal of Politics* had long conversations before the launch about how to create a new journal that would be academically and intellectually (these are not necessarily synonymous) serious, respected, and valued, while at the same time did not reproduce some of the traits they had all come to see as hallmarks of masculinized academic-journal-editing practice—a practice that narrows and dampens the knowledge sharing required to do serious gender research on international relations. Here are a few things they together decided would be necessary if the *International Feminist Journal of Politics* were to achieve both of these ambitious goals.

First, the journal headquarters would have to be located outside the United States as often as possible. This decision came out of a recognition that in today's globalized academic world, American universities, publishers, and scholars play a disproportionate role due to the dominance of English, the size of the country, the number of its universities and colleges, the predominance of U.S. foreign policy actions throughout most regions of the world, and the economic power of U.S.-based media. Thus, while American academics serve as members of the editorial advisory board, contribute articles, and occasionally serve as one of the trio of chief editors, the headquarters was located first in Australia, then in Britain, and then in Canada. Only in its fourth round of editors was it headquartered at an American university.

Second, the journal's founding group decided that there would be three chief editors, rotating every three years, and that these editors would always come from three different geographic regions. Third, the group decided that "blind" reviewers would give suggestions and criticisms of all submitted articles in a spirit of collegial helpfulness. The founders also wanted submissions from young scholars to be encouraged. Fourth, the founders decided that the journal would welcome potential articles from any academic field that sheds light on the ways in which international relations becomes gendered. The journal would "toss overboard" the common assumption that scholars trained in political science are the only ones who can show us how the international system works—and why.

The multinational group of founders made another important decision: this journal would not shy away from a feminist identity. "Feminist" would be printed in bold letters as part of the new journal's title. On the other hand, the journal would not adopt a static, parochial, or single definition of "feminist," because the founders all had learned how place-, time-, and culture-specific feminist analyses can be.

Finally, during these lively discussions in the mid-1990s—discussions that produced what they hoped would become a new kind of forum for the serious investigation of international politics—the journal's founders decided that every issue would contain a featured section called "Conversations," a place where alternative forms of serious intellectual discussion of "international politics" could appear—interviews, conference reports, even film reviews. That is, they recognized that globalizing politics occurs in many arenas, not just inside governments or within international agencies.

Integral to all of these intellectual endeavors by feminist scholars has been challenging the long-established, conventional concept of—and explanations for—"national security." The hunch has been that if we think outside the "state security box," if we take seriously the lives of women—their diverse understandings of security—as well as the on-the-ground workings of masculinity and femininity, we will be able to produce more meaningful and more reliable analyses of "security"—personal, national, and global (Hansen and Olsson 2004).

By employing a feminist curiosity—that is, by asking (and seeking to answer) hard questions about diverse women's relationships to men, to the nation, to the state, and to other women, as well as questions about how men's relationships to diverse notions of masculinity affect women's lives and the operations of politics—scholars and teachers are seeking to get a more realistic and less militarized understanding of what "security" means now and what it could potentially mean in the future. These scholars are discovering that ideas (and policies) about masculinity and about femininity are frequently the consequence of "national security" doctrines—for example, that the more militarized the criteria adopted for national security, the more it is only men who are presumed to be those most trusted to handle foreign policymaking, and that anyone imagined to be "feminine" is often deemed unsuited for the "hard" thinking involved in this realm called national security.

On the other hand, ideas about masculinity and femininity might be the cause of national security choices. That is, as we saw in the case of globalized sneaker politics, when we use a feminist curiosity we can shine a searchlight not just on impacts but also on causality.

Take the ongoing investigations into why the U.S. government under several presidents pursued military solutions to political problems in the small Southeast Asian country of Vietnam so persistently. In the summer of 2004, Daniel Ellsberg was still puzzling about this. As a young man in 1971, Daniel Ellsberg was working under contract for the U.S. Defense Department. He became a hero to many and a traitor in the eyes of some when he secretly photocopied hundreds of pages of an in-house government report analyzing the policy failures of the United States in waging its war in Vietnam. President Richard Nixon failed in his attempts to convince the Supreme Court that national security necessity made it legal to stop the public release of the damning report. The report, read by millions of Americans and people around the world after it was published in the *New York Times* and the *Washington Post*, became known as the *Pentagon Papers*. In 2004, more than three decades later, Daniel Ellsberg was still wondering why Nixon's predecessor, Lyndon B. Johnson, so stubbornly persisted in waging a war that even his closest advisors were telling him was unwinnable and was growing deeply unpopular among many Americans.

Ellsberg, speaking to a group of peace-activist military veterans in July 2004, wondered out loud what motivated President Johnson's refusal to back down from his failing war-waging policy. After years of thinking about this question and weighing all the alternative answers, Ellsberg told his audience that he had come to the conclusion that it was not President Johnson's anticommunist ideology and not his famous electoral calculations. Rather, Ellsberg had concluded, it was President Johnson's fear of being feminized, that is, of being "unmanly." Ellsberg had become convinced that this American president's anxiety was fueled by his imagining that if he backed away from a military engagement, he would open himself to charges of being, in American slang, a "wimp"—of not having the masculine credentials to see a country through a war, even a failed and unpopular war.

The jury is still out regarding why presidents Lyndon Johnson and Richard Nixon were so persistent in their commitment to a U.S. military engagement in Vietnam, in which over 50,000 U.S. soldiers and thousands more Vietnamese—and Cambodian and Laotian—soldiers and civilians died. But it is worth taking seriously Daniel Ellsberg's carefully considered argument. Which of the many militarized foreign policy decisions made by any senior government official in any country is affected even in part by their personal worries about not appearing "feminine"?

Gender analysts use a similar feminist curiosity to investigate the experiences of the international civilian weapons inspectors sent to Iraq by the United Nations in 2002. This was a highly masculinized team— that is, it was widely believed within the United Nations and the UN Security Council that only men had the sorts of attitudes and technical expertise appropriate to conduct this politically loaded international scientific weapons inspection. Nonetheless, despite its conformity to the conventions of masculinized international security affairs, the team, headed by Swedish diplomat Hans Blix, had its findings repeatedly challenged by the Bush administration in the months of tense UN debates leading up to the eventual U.S. preemptive military invasion of Iraq in March 2003.

Feminist scholar Carol Cohn wondered why. She decided to dig more deeply into this international politics of weapons inspection and its failure of credibility at such a critical moment in the evolving post–Cold War global politics of security. After all, the United Nations was created in 1945 to help roll back global militarization, to make wars less likely. Why had it seemingly failed in March 2003?

Cohn and her co-researchers, Felicity Hill and Sara Ruddick, were invited in 2005 to Stockholm to present their analysis of the international politics of weapons inspections to the members of the prestigious Weapons of Mass Destruction Commission (WMDC). The audience, composed of former ambassadors, senior UN officials, and former secretaries and ministers of defense, also included Hans Blix himself. Most of the people there in the hall that day were quite new to feminist analysis (Cohn, Hill, and Ruddick 2005).

Here is what Cohn, Ruddick, and Hill reported to their rather skeptical Stockholm listeners. The internationally heated debate during 2002 and early 2003 was over whether the government of President Saddam Hussein was developing weapons of mass destruction, as President George W. Bush and his advisors were contending—and which contentions were being made the basis for developing elaborate plans for a U.S.-led military invasion of Iraq to topple the Saddam Hussein regime. The Hans Blix team reported back to the UN Security Council that its months of on-site inspections had turned up no evidence that the Iraqi government had an active program of developing weapons of mass destruction. The Bush administration, speaking to its own American legislators and citizens, as well as to its co-members of the UN Security Council, dismissed the Blix team's findings as not credible, thus justifying its own continued buildup for a military invasion and its pressure on the governments of Britain, Australia, Spain, the Ukraine, Japan, Italy, and Honduras to commit their own troops to a U.S.-led military invasion.

Credibility turned out to be the principal currency in what had become a high-stakes and potentially deadly global game. Credibility is in the eyes of the beholders. Earning credibility is almost always shaped by the workings of gender (Enloe 2013).

Carol Cohn and her co-investigators shined a feminist curiosity light on political credibility. What creates it? What undermines it? In whose eyes? They discovered that the Bush administration repeatedly cast doubt on the credibility of mere diplomats. The powerful strand of American political culture that values manly shows of overt strength over allegedly "softer" or more feminized demonstrations of patient, careful negotiations had become even more dominant in the wake of the attacks of September 11, 2001. Thus, in various public settings, the Bush administration portrayed the civilian UN inspectors as somehow less trustworthy and less credible because they were following a course of action that was less committed to a demonstration of physical force. The drama of the months leading up to the U.S. military invasion of Iraq was a contest between masculinities.

The largely male audience in Stockholm listening to Cohn, Hill, and Ruddick's analysis were not immediately convinced. Most of the audience had never thought it necessary to develop the skills with which to conduct a feminist analysis of international or national security. Yet when Carol Cohn met one of the prominent members of the WMDC several months later, he went out of his way to tell her that he had continued to think about her talk and about the role that competing ideas about masculinity had played in the political contest between the UN weapons inspectors and the Bush administration. And, he admitted, he had begun to think for the first time that ideas about, and demonstrations of, masculinity may have been decisive in the final Security Council outcome.

When it came to writing their two hundred-page annual report, members of the WMDC inserted just one short paragraph indicating that gendered analysis was starting to make an impact on their collective thinking:

> Women have rightly observed that armament policies and the use of armed force have often been influenced by the misguided ideas about masculinity and strength. An understanding of and emancipation from this traditional perspective might help to remove some of the hurdles on the road to disarmament and non-proliferation. (Weapons of Mass Destruction Commission 2006, 160)

A postscript: According to one WMDC commissioner, this brief nod to gendered analysis did not get inserted by the commission into its report because of a broad consensus among the members that gender matters. Rather, this commissioner confidentially recalled, a reference to the influence of the politics of masculinity on global nuclear, chemical, and biological weapons proliferation went into the report only at the insistence of one of the few women on the commission, an experienced international civil servant. Had she not been in the room, the insights offered by Cohn, Hill, and Ruddick might never have gotten into print.

This web of experiences suggests that a brief flash of gendered understanding on the parts of men and women whose professional careers have depended on not acknowledging the impacts of femininity and masculinity will not be sustained—for instance, in ongoing international diplomatic political discussions with the governments of Iran and North Korea—if there aren't persistent institutional encouragements and affirmations to support that initial flash of understanding. Ideas matter. But ideas need to be nurtured by formal and informal social (including institutional) dynamics. One of the reasons that ungendered explanations of militarization are so persistent is that they are the explanations that—when offered at a closed meeting or over supper or in a public debate—are treated as "rational," "serious," and "sophisticated."

Asking feminist questions in the study of national and global security, thus, includes asking the following questions about masculinity:

- Who holds what views of manliness?
- Who wields those ideas in political life?
- What are the consequences of those views and ideas?

Investigating all three questions also requires keeping a close eye on femininity: who fears it, why, and with what results.

The answers in any particular circumstance aren't preordained. Taking the questions seriously and crafting strategies to pursue them carefully will make us smarter.

As these two cases suggest, militarization of global affairs is likely to be propelled forward by masculinization and by certain players' fears of feminization. Like globalization and militarization, the processes of feminization and masculinization should be investigated as step-by-step processes. To make sense of any process—globalization, militarization, masculinization, feminization—we again need to stay alert over time, to operate like a historian, not a photographer.

Masculinization, as we have seen, often is fueled by key players' anxieties and fears of feminization. Indian policymakers, for instance, have pursued nuclear weapons acquisition in part out of the conviction that India is feminized in world affairs and that acquiring nuclear weapons will reverse that allegedly humiliating process (Oza 2006; Sitaraman 2007). Any person or group of people who think that if they are perceived to be "feminine" they will lose political influence, credibility, or respect, are likely to take steps to avoid being perceived that way: they will stay quiet about their genuine reservations; they might speak publicly about the values of strength and decisive threatening action; they will make clear that they personally are always ready to wield military might; they might even cast doubt on the manliness of those who are criticizing military solutions (diplomats, pacifists, "the French") (Conway 2012).

Masculinization can proceed part way and then be resisted and stalled. Thus, one needs to monitor—and explain—every step along the way. This means that we need to use our feminist curiosity to explain how and why any state's notion of "national security" has become militarized or masculinized to a large degree or only to a lesser degree. But we won't uncover the answers if we ignore or trivialize the lives of women.

When I first started trying to make sense of security policy, I thought that I needed just two concepts in my analytical toolbox: "militarism" and "the military." The first—"militarism"—was a package of distinct but interdependent values and beliefs about how the world "works" and how the world ought to work. The second concept—"the military"—was meant to distinguish a particular sort of institution. According to this concept, a military was distinct from a family, a baseball team, a political party, a corporation, or a police force. I thought that, equipped with these two concepts, I could adequately shed an explanatory light on national and international security politics.

I was wrong. What I slowly began to realize was that relying on the concepts of "militarism" and "militaries" would not enable me to explain how the politics of what was defined as "national," and what was defined as "security" might change from one decade to another. In other words, with only the flashlights of "militarism" and "military" in my toolbox, I could see parts of the room but not enough of it to build a satisfactory explanation for how the world actually works. I found that I could not understand how in any given society—Nigeria, Sudan, Cambodia, Syria, Sweden, Colombia, Egypt, Israel, the United States, Argentina—militarism, that package of beliefs and values, had come to gain a foothold: How could this particular package of ideas have been weak in the past yet later become so strong that most elites and many ordinary citizens imagined that "national security" and militarism were synonymous?

"Militarism" was a useful concept, but not useful enough. It turned out to be too static. I could measure popular and elite ideas against it, but I could not explain how and why changes in either popular or elite presumptions had been transformed over a year, a decade, or a generation. I found that I wanted to explain the politics of national security—to expose its causes. Why did that person—or that political party or that agency—in an effort to achieve national security, become more dependent on militaristic strategies? Why then? Why not earlier? Why not later?

Adopting militarization as a conceptual tool, I also became curious about the broader politics of things most of my political science colleagues dismissed back then as not really "political": the politics of marriage, of fear, of workplace morale, of identity. And I then discovered that I could not adequately explore any of these political concepts unless I took diverse women seriously.

At this point in my development, I started to pay close attention to the smart research of other feminists on schemes by war planners, military juntas, and defense administrators to control women—efforts to control women's fears, women's ambitions, women's sense of belonging, women's sexuality, and women's labor. Works by feminist historians investigating World Wars I and II began to crowd out the more conventional political science books on my shelves. I also began reading a lot more works by anthropologists because they had developed tools to track cultural meanings.

I started to attend panel sessions at conferences on popular culture and on cross-cultural constructions of femininity. I changed the sort of assignments I gave students in my seminars. Now I urged each student to do an in-depth interview with any woman—of any age, any class, any nationality—to see if that woman had ever been dependent on, influenced by, or controlled by a military. The goal was not to judge that woman, but to understand her experiences. As they each tried to make sense of the life of just one woman, these attentive student researchers revealed that militarization was a subtle, nuanced, even confusing, sometimes sporadic, and often contested process.

Militarized wives: One student interviewed her sister-in-law. She chose her because she wondered what impact it had on her to be married to her own brother, who was a weapons engineer. Although both her sister-in-law and brother were civilians, this student discovered through her careful interviewing that their marriage gradually had become militarized. Her sister-in-law recalled how when they first got together, they had lively conversations about politics, including about Russia, a country she had always found fascinating. But, as their marriage progressed, she became aware that her husband was becoming uncomfortable with those sorts of conversations. Furthermore, she gradually realized that there were whole areas of his work life at the defense contracting company that were "out of bounds," that he could not discuss and that she should not ask about. Over time, a sea of silence opened up in their marriage. They were both civilians, but their married life had become militarized. To sustain their marriage, she would have to become an un-inquisitive wife.

Civilian women who become the wives of civilian men working—often as scientists and technical specialists—in tight communities dominated by a secret weapons projects find their lives are even more intensely militarized. Three such towns have been: Livermore, California, home of nuclear weapons research facilities, Livermore Laboratories; Richland, Washington, home of the plutonium research and production facility, the Hanford plutonium plant; and Ozersk, serving Russia's Maiak plutonium plant in the Urals region of southern Russia. Livermore, Richland, and Ozersk became home to scores of families living what in each country seemed to be idealized middle-class suburban lives: good schools, good housing, good pay, and apparent security.

Each of these towns was a company town, that is, dependent on and controlled by a single employer. In the case of these three towns, the central government was the principal (in Richland and Ozersk, the sole) employer. In Richland, DuPont, a large chemical corporation, served as the U.S. government's chief contractor. Each of these profoundly militarized towns was created out of its chief employer's national security-justified racialized, ethnicized, classed, and gendered imaginings—imaginings of skill, obedience, reliability, and loyalty (Brown 2013; Gusterson 1996).

While there were women employed in all three of these weapons facilities, managers routinely hired women as lower-paid, less-influential technicians; these same managers, themselves men, made decisions that masculinized the senior scientific posts and administrative positions. For the women making their lives as civilian wives in all three of these militarized civilian towns, the national security price they were asked by their respective governments to pay in return for the seeming comforts and amenities they enjoyed in each town was the surrender of their individual judgment and curiosity. That is, these civilian wives were expected not to act and think as full-fledged citizens (Brown 2013; Gusterson 1996). To the extent that any of these women decided that it was a fair bargain—and many wives did make this choice—they became militarized. Their governments' national security strategists were counting on them to accept this marital bargain.

Military wives: Civilian women who are married to uniformed male soldiers (and now, in some countries, civilian women married to women soldiers) seem far away from the pinnacles of state power. Nevertheless, we gain a valuable insight into the workings of militarization if we pay serious attention to those women who are married to the state's soldiers and possess little political influence.

By applying a gender analysis, we reveal that masculinized government officials in many countries spend a lot of time, resources, and energy trying to socialize and control those women who have married their state's soldiers. We also learn that many women have found satisfaction and rewards in trying to live up to the government's—and their husband's—expectations. Many civilian women married to soldiers have been able to see themselves as genuine patriots for doing all that the government needs them to do:

- moving frequently
- sacrificing their own career aspirations
- volunteering for unpaid work to knit a military base community together
- enduring the loneliness of single motherhood when their soldier/ husbands are deployed far away
- staying publicly cheerful while privately coping with their husband/soldiers' bouts of anger and depression after stints in tense combat zones
- not asking too many questions about the possible sexual liaisons their husbands might have engaged in when away from home
- staying stoically quiet in their grief if their husbands are killed while deployed

Some women gain in social and economic status by marrying a soldier, especially if he earns promotions, moving up through the ranks of the military's officer corps. As a bonus, some women married to soldiers like the close community they experience on a military base, and they take pride in their children's capacity to adapt to new environments (Alva 2006; Hyde 2015).

On the other hand, some women married to soldiers have refused to conform to the official expectations of how the proper military wife should behave—for instance, by encouraging their husbands not to reenlist, by speaking out about domestic violence perpetrated by soldier-husbands and soldier-boyfriends against their wives and girl-friends, by criticizing the policies that deprive senior officers' wives of military health care and housing benefits when their husbands file for divorce, despite the years of service many of these women have contributed to the community life on military bases, or (hardest of all) by speaking out as the civilians when they disagree with their government's foreign policy.

When military wives take any of these unusual steps, officials get nervous. They try to brush domestic violence inside military families under the rug. They try to provide benefits to war widows. They publicly portray the entire military as a "family." They enlist other military wives as the chief socializers of women who have recently married soldiers. Despite all this effort, however, in many policymaking settings, military officials commonly may act as though military wives are a bother, a distraction from the military's primary mission (Alvarez 2006; Enloe 2010; Eran-Jona 2005; Harrison 2002; Harrison and Laliberte 1994; Houppert 2005; Hyde 2015; Lutz 2001; Ware 2012; Zahedi 2006).

Civilian women married to soldiers, learning to admire a militarized form of masculinity in their husbands and complying with their government's own models of militarized marriage, therefore, are integral to those governments' preferred "national security" doctrines.

When we try to explain any government official's masculinized "national security" policies, we are tempted to imagine that these women married to soldiers are a trivial concern. "Trivial" is worth pausing to think about. We tend to pay little attention to anything that can be dismissed as trivial. Behind that dismissive attitude are the beliefs that women married to soldiers scarcely wield influence with their own husbands and that women married to soldiers have no impact on ideas about technology or enemies or allies or violence. Another trivializing assumption is that women married to soldiers are of no concern to state planners because they are just women "doing what comes naturally." For anything that happens naturally—a woman going along with whatever career choices her husband made and with the daily consequences of her husband's career choice—seems unworthy of serious investigation.

No one, however, is born an obedient, flexible, loyal, patriotic woman, a woman who loves swinging back and forth between living sometimes like a grateful dependent and other times like a resourceful single parent. A woman has to be persuaded, and sometimes is pressured, to become—and stay—a "model military wife." The design and implementation of those persuasion and pressure techniques has been an unexamined part of governments' "national security" operations.

That is, if too many women married to soldiers rebel—divorce their soldier-husbands or refuse to revert to grateful dependency after having spent months crafting the skills of independent lone parenthood, or start talking to journalists of their doubts about the government's foreign policies—many officials see those women not simply as falling short of a feminized militarized marital ideal but as threats to national security. Such women come to be seen by commanders (and sometimes other more pro-government military wives) as "problem wives," insofar as their actions might weaken the morale of soldier-husbands or might weaken popular resolve to accept the costs of the government's policies. Precisely because it is so popularly imagined that military wives are "naturally" patriotic and that their patriotism will take the form of accepting what their government's officials need from both them and their husbands, when military wives do speak out critically, their opinions attract attention—and often harsh criticism.

Researcher Monica Henry heard women married to American soldiers describe their fears about speaking out when she interviewed them during the U.S.-led war in Iraq. Many military wives told Henry that they supported the U.S. government's invasion and occupation of Iraq, explaining to her that their trust in the president, their support of the president's foreign policy in Iraq, and their loyalty to their husbands deployed to Iraq were all of a single piece. Yet those military wives who had become critical of the war said it was very risky to voice their opinions out loud: if a military wife spoke out, military commanders could hear of it and perhaps hinder her husband's career; the military wife herself might be ostracized by other military wives, on whose support she may depend during her husband's months overseas; an outspoken military wife might find her on-base job jeopardized. As one longtime military wife, who used the Internet pseudonym "Love My Tanker," told Henry, "Although it doesn't say this anywhere in any regulations, etc., if I am a problem wife, the chain of command will know about it. . . . Everything I do or do not do, say or do not say, could have an impact on my husband. . . . The military is actually a small place" (Henry 2006, 46).

Suddenly the topic of women married to soldiers no longer looks "trivial."

Trivializing tendencies when considering diverse women has made it harder to devote attention to the gendered intellectual presumptions of those engaged in the study of national and international security. It is not surprising, then, that it has been "outsiders"—researchers and teachers using a feminist curiosity—who have pushed open creaking doors, raised dusty windows, and shone new light into dimly lit rooms, and who have thereby provided a fresh alternative to the older masculinized and militarized menu of topics and questions to delve into as we seek a clearer understanding of "national security" politics.

One of the most powerful ideas that makes the militarization of national security seem "natural" (i.e., not worth questioning) is the notion that there is an allegedly "natural" relationship between the protected and the protector—inside of families, on military bases, in societies at large. It takes a feminist curiosity and gender-analysis skills to lift up these two heavy rocks of national security studies and policymaking so we can critically scrutinize what ideas lie under both of them. Conventional ideas about this protected-protector relationship appear to perpetuate the political assumption that in any community some people are naturally the protectors while others are naturally the protected.

Going against the grain of this conventional wisdom, historians studying marriage and girls' education, sociologists examining family law, activists trying to stop domestic violence, women's studies researchers investigating military conscription, and feminist labor activists together have given us an alternative understanding of the politics of the protector and protected and have revealed just how pervasive this gendered protector-protected system has become. They also have exposed the extent to which this widespread assumption can distort power relations: it is much easier to claim the authority to speak for others if one can claim to be The Protector; it is much easier to be silenced and to accept that silencing if one absorbs the self-identity of The Protected.

We have only begun to apply this critical analysis of socially constructed protection to the field of "national security." In applying this feminist knowledge to national security politics, we are rejecting the belief that our knowledge about the history of marriage, of child custody, of divorce, and of domestic violence is relevant "only" to the local arenas of public affairs. Instead, we are showing that a feminist historian of marriage (or of education or of violence against women) is indeed exactly the right "expert" to place on a panel to discuss nuclear weapons proliferation. We are demonstrating that useful, eye-opening discussions of foreign policy and military influences will result from exactly this sort of intellectual conversation.

An allegedly "natural" protector is the person who has not just the physical strength or the collective physical resources to wield definitive power, but who also—allegedly—is the person most capable of thinking in a certain useful way: more "strategically," more "rationally." The protectors are those who can see beyond the minutiae of daily life— those who have the ability to see the Big Picture. In any patriarchal society, the protectors are deemed to be the most worldly, and thus natural controllers of the feminized protected not merely because they are stronger than the protected but because they are (allegedly) smarter. They can act "for their own good." The masculinization of national security studies and of national security policymaking depends on ideas about who is feminized. This process of masculinization, therefore, flows directly out of the patriarchal belief that one has to be "manly" in order to be rational enough to be responsible for the security of "women and children."

For the protectors to wield this public superiority, there must be a certain constructed "protected." The protected is the allegedly feminized person who is not at ease in the public sphere. The protected's natural habitat is the domestic sphere—that is, the sphere of life where caring matters more than strategizing. Consequently, the protected is feminized insofar as the protected needs somebody who can think strategically and act in her (the protected's) best interests. This masculinization of the protector and its necessary feminization of the protected has far-reaching implications. First, such a process of masculinization justifies state secrecy. The most "manly" state policymakers and their academic advisors are the only ones rational enough to keep secrets. Less manly (i.e., less rational, less strategically "tough-minded") men—most (not all) elected legislators, most civil servants working in the more feminized departments of the state (e.g., health, culture, environment), most (not all) male journalists—and virtually all women can be excluded from the "top secret" inner circles of national security.

Today, with militarizing processes in so many countries in high gear, it is more urgent than ever to be curious about how this relationship between the alleged protectors and the alleged protected depends on questionable assumptions about masculinities and femininities. To put that curiosity into investigatory action, one will have to be equipped with the tools of gender analysis.

Doing that gender analysis of militarizing processes will clarify what must be done by those who want to propel effective *de*-militarization.

Those who now claim to be the nation's protectors have a stake in portraying the world as (and turning the world into) a "dangerous place." If we direct our feminist flashlights to the processes of making and justifying national security policies, we will find that state elites—with the help of media editors, academic consultants, technical experts, and husbands—invest a lot of effort in keeping afloat this artificial, unequal relationship between the masculinized protectors and the feminized protected.

But we will also discover that this politically charged relationship is frequently challenged, even if those challenging actions are ignored by most media. When peace activists women hold up signs at their vigils declaring "Not in Our Name!" they are deliberately disrupting the patriarchal masculinized protector–feminized protected dichotomy on which most "national security" systems are built.

Women in many countries who have made "Not in Our Name!" their own political declaration are proclaiming that they are not merely the narrowly imagined, feminized protected. They are citizens.

CHAPTER 5

PAYING CLOSE ATTENTION TO WOMEN *INSIDE* MILITARIES

The woman soldier. This used to be an oxymoron. Even if there were tales of women acting heroically in warfare (think of Joan of Arc, think of the Amazons), they were deemed anomalous or just fanciful. In the mid-twentieth century, women as armed combatants in insurgent forces—in China, Vietnam, Algeria, Nicaragua, El Salvador, Mozambique, Zimbabwe, Eritrea, and the Philippines—became more visible.

By the early years of the twenty-first century, the woman soldier seemed to have become a globalized icon of the "modern woman." She was breaking feminized taboos, entering a traditionally masculinized domain, being deployed far from home, displaying her physical strength, handling high-tech weaponry. She was defying the strictures of conventional, patriarchal femininity by proving that she could be the protector, not simply the protected—she, like a manly man, could "die for her country." To some, the woman soldier was thereby showing that a woman could be a "first-class citizen" in her own country and a militarized "peacekeeper" around the world.

During the post-2011 devastating wars in Syria and Iraq, most of the armed fighting forces on the ground, regardless of their competing political goals, reverted to virtually all-male organizations. The Iraqi Shiite militias, the Islamic State (ISIS) forces, the rival Islamic-identified foreign fighters' insurgent militias, and the more secular Syrian anti-government forces—the leaders of each made masculinization their core organizing principle. The exceptions were the Turkish and Iraqi Kurdish insurgent forces, both of whose male leaders incorporated a significant number of women as fighters. In this Syrian/Iraqi conflict, however, women were valued and recruited in order to play support roles, chiefly as male fighters' loyal wives (Callimachi 2015; Jaffer 2015).

By contrast, at the same time, on the global landscape of state militaries the woman soldier was appearing everywhere. She was smiling out from a Japanese Self-Defense Forces recruiting advertisement; she was looking boldly at you from the Swedish military's website; she was marching in Vietnam's patriotic veterans' parades; she was fighting in Syria with her Kurdish militia comrades; she was donning the UN's blue helmet on an international peacekeeping mission; she was on patrol in Afghanistan with NATO forces; she was singing the national anthem at an American sporting event; as a wounded veteran, she was showing off the agility of her prosthetic arm (Eager 2014; Enloe 2010; Kronsell 2012; Mackenzie 2012, 2015; Sato 2012; Turner 1998).

There seemed to be a halo of modernity glowing around this woman soldier. The pursuit of modernity is one of the incentives that governments and individuals find appealing for joining the process of globalization. For some people today, no military can claim to be a genuinely "modern military" unless it allows at least some women to join its ranks. In the late 1990s, Italy was the last of all the NATO countries to permit women to enlist. The all-male military seemed to be going the way of the all-male college. Today there are women soldiers in the militaries ranging from those of Saudi Arabia, Kuwait, India, South Africa, and North Korea, to those of Norway, South Korea, Colombia, Nepal, Fiji, and China. Modernity, that pot of gold at the end of the globalized rainbow, has demanded that at least some women be permitted access to soldiering.

This iconic image of the woman soldier was reminiscent of an earlier globalized image of the modern woman. She was popularly called—and often proudly called herself—the "New Woman." During the 1910s and 1920s, she too popped up all over the world. In cities such as Istanbul, Cairo, Seoul, Shanghai, Tokyo, Paris, Chicago, Toronto, and London, she was the young woman who left her small town and migrated to the city. As a New Woman, she thrived on the lively bustle and seeming freedom of the big city. She wanted to experience independence, earning her own wages in an office job and living with women friends in a boarding house or rented apartment, away from the confines of family supervision. The New Woman dressed in newly relaxed fashions and read books and slick magazines written for her and about her. She resisted marriage until it could be on her own terms. In many places she was exercising her newly won right to vote; in some places she was joining with other women to create public campaigns to open up new opportunities for women (Ito 2006; Ito and Morimoto 2004; Kwon 2000).

Some of these New Women were, just as some of the contemporary women soldiers are, feminists; that is, they deliberately analyzed, critiqued, and collectively challenged the power systems that operated daily to keep women socially confined, physically constrained, economically dependent, and politically sidelined. Many other women who earlier aspired to become New Women or who today enlist in the military, however, eschew feminism. These women, though adventurous, have been afraid that if they are seen by their colleagues or the general public as "feminists," they will have a harder time achieving their own unconventional personal goals.

The contemporary woman soldier and the earlier New Woman each was the object of popular hope and admiration. But, not surprisingly, each was—and still is—the target of intense debate and even scorn, since both the woman soldier and the New Woman—even if they did or do not embrace the label "feminist"—undermined assumptions about biology, respectability, and femininity. These women thereby raised new discomforting questions about the roles, skills, and privileges of men.

The New Woman was a globalizing phenomenon. Women in Seoul traveled to Tokyo to meet and study with those Japanese women writers and artists whose liberated lives they admired. Women in China and Japan translated and put on productions of Norwegian playwright

Henrik Ibsen's controversial play "A Doll's House," which portrays one woman's rebellion against her claustrophobic middle-class marriage (Weinbaum et al. 2008).

So too today women in militaries often—not always—develop a global awareness and create their own international networks. They are keen to find out what is going on in the lives of women soldiers in other countries. They meet and compare notes when they are deployed on joint peacekeeping operations, when they travel abroad for special training courses, or when they gather for conferences sponsored by various advocacy groups to discuss the continuing barriers women soldiers face when seeking promotions or simply respect: "Are you allowed to serve in combat roles?" "Do your superiors ignore women's complaints of sexual harassment?" "How have you managed to get your veterans' hospitals to offer services that address women's reproductive health issues?" (Manning 2006).

For all their intriguing similarities, however, the globalized New Woman of the 1910s and 1920s and today's globalized woman soldier are marked by a major difference. The New Woman was typically the object of contempt and even fear (she was tearing apart the nation, she was a traitor to the nationalist cause, she was upsetting the "social order"). By stark contrast, women in today's state militaries—if they stay in the roles their commanders assign them—are there because government strategists think they will enhance, not subvert, "national security":

(a) they will make up for the loss of middle-class men caused by the repeal of male conscription laws ("the draft"),

(b) they will compensate for a decline in the country's birthrate (because many women are having fewer babies than they did a generation ago),

(c) they will allow the government not to recruit "too many" men from those ethnic and racial groups the government's elite doesn't respect or trust,

(d) they will bring with them higher levels of formal education than many of the country's young men achieve,

(e) they can be assigned to search local women in Afghanistan without upsetting conservative mores,

(f) they will help make the government's military look "modern" in the eyes of many of its own citizens and observers abroad.

As was true of the earlier New Women, these women inside today's militaries provoke mixed responses, both admiration and anxiety. Each group of women can benefit their countries, many observers seem to imply, *only if* their energies and talents can be controlled in ways that direct them to fulfilling the government's goals.

The "only if" matters. Such conditions can be tough to sustain when women in any military start making alliances with supportive civilian legislators or civil society advocates, or when the military is stretched thin and needs to open up loopholes to make maximum use of all personnel—male and female; young and old; gay, transgender, and straight; racially privileged and racially marginalized. Thus, during the 2001–2016 U.S.-led wars in Afghanistan and Iraq, observers have noted that, despite denials by senior officials that American women were in "combat"—the hallowed role reserved for generations solely for "manly" men—in practice, women soldiers deployed to both Iraq and Afghanistan were routinely assigned by field commanders to combat operations (Eager 2014; Enloe 2010; Mackenzie 2015; Solaro 2006).

What can we investigate, then, by taking seriously women soldiers in any military? First, we can determine whether many women are joining military forces because they believe it is the route to "first-class citizenship." If we find out that they are, then paying attention to women soldiers becomes a strategy for analyzing the militarization of citizenship. Second, we can discover whether, in the civilian public's eyes, women serving as soldiers are becoming symbols of the country's "modernity." If they are, then taking women in the military seriously will enable us to chart the militarization of globalized modernity. Third, we can determine whether the growing numbers of women soldiers in the military's ranks are persuading more and more civilians that their own country's military is no longer sexist. If we find that that is so, then our conducting a gender analysis of militaries' recruitment of women will help us understand how ongoing patriarchy can be camouflaged.

Paying attention to women soldiers takes stamina. It entails watching the recruitment strategies and rationales of a government over several decades. It simultaneously requires listening to women soldiers themselves, women from diverse ethnic and racial and socioeconomic backgrounds. For instance, during the 1990s and early 2000s, African American women constituted a surprisingly high percentage of all active-duty women enlisted in the U.S. Army—that is, four times the percentage of African American women among all women in the general U.S. population (Manning 2005). Since 2000, however, the percentage of African American women among enlisted-rank military women has been dropping—from a high of 48 percent in the early 1990s, to 38 percent in 2005, to 31 percent in 2011. This, of course, still is almost three times their proportion of all women in the United States. Furthermore, it is a significantly higher percentage than African American men (16 percent) are of all U.S. military men (Patten 2011).

In other words, paying attention to women soldiers does not mean homogenizing them. Instead, it entails taking seriously the unequal tendencies of young women in different racial and ethnic groups within the same society to join their country's military. Is an Afro-Colombian young woman as likely to be attracted by the Colombian recruiter's appeal as a mestizo Colombian young woman? Is a Bangladeshi British young woman as likely to sign up for the British Army as a white British young woman?

Moreover, once diverse women join any military, they may have quite different experiences as soldiers. Training opportunities and promotions may not be equally distributed across women of all backgrounds. All women may not be equally subjected to sexual harassment from male sergeants and officers. Reactions to serving on peacekeeping missions, for instance, in the Congo, South Sudan, or the Sinai, may not be identical for women soldiers of all social backgrounds within the same country's contingent. As always, being a gender analyst requires being constantly curious about the inter-workings of gender with those of class, race, and ethnicity.

"Paying attention" as a curious gender analyst also requires listening to silences. When women inside any military (or any military academy) do not report sexual abuse perpetrated by their male colleagues and superiors—because they decide the military justice system cannot be trusted, because they fear being ostracized as "turncoats" by their peers, or because they have seen how other women's careers have been harmed after they have spoken up—that is significant. It takes courage in any patriarchal institution to raise public objections to masculinized abuse. Thus, for instance, one might pay close attention to the more than one hundred young women in the United States who spoke up during 2005 alone, charging that male military recruiters—from all services—sexually harassed them while in the process of trying to enlist them. At the U.S. Army military academy West Point in 2014, of all the women cadets, 55 percent said that they had experienced sexual harassment at the academy (U.S. Department of Defense, 2015). Perhaps it was somehow easier for these young women to break the silence because they were still civilians and not yet officially in the military. Or perhaps they were able to speak out because most of them still lived at home and had older adults, their parents, to give them support when they reported their experiences.

Women already serving in the British military, for instance, have expressed little confidence that, if they speak out about their experiences of sexual harassment or assault, they will be supported by their superiors or treated justly. They believe that the military's institutional culture tilts toward privileging masculinity in ways that will discredit their charges (Basham 2013; Buchanan 2015). In one case that came to the British courts, Corporal Leah Mates, a thirty-year-old soldier with extensive professional military experience, reported being subjected to repeated sexual bullying. When her supervisors treated her reports of the behavior dismissively, Corporal Mates testified, "I now began to understand that the Army is a male preserve, and a woman who tries to establish herself does so at the peril of her health and happiness" (Maley 2006).

In the United States in recent years, women's advocacy groups outside the military, such as the U.S.-based Service Women's Action Network (SWAN), have organized to provide women inside the military support and validation when they dare to speak out about sexual violence and abuse in the ranks. When the Defense Department's officials still have not listened, these activists have pushed members of Congress to take their words seriously (www.servicewomen.org).

"Paying attention," furthermore, calls for listening to civilians—boyfriends, girlfriends, husbands, mothers, fathers, teachers, journalists, elected officials, movie directors, civilian women and men in those countries to which women soldiers are deployed. Each group of observers weighs the rightness and consequences of the women in their lives serving in militaries. For instance, a father who is a military veteran may see his daughter's enlistment as carrying on "the family tradition"—especially if his son does not want to join the military. On the other hand, a civilian boyfriend might start worrying that if he and his soldier-girlfriend get married and she stays in the military, he will end up like a military wife, acting as a single parent for months while she is deployed overseas.

The percentage of women in the military in various countries in 2010–2015 is shown in table 5.1.

We need to treat these percentages with caution. Even the relatively high percentages might not be evidence of contemporary "post-sexist" enlightenment. The percentage of women in any country's military may wax and wane over time. For instance, during World War II, the U.S. government deliberately recruited thousands of women—white, African American, Chinese, Japanese, Latina, Native American—to join the Navy's WAVES, the Army's WAC, and the Coast Guard's SPARS, which were branches of the military created by the wartime government especially for women. After the war ended, male officials in the White House, the War Department (then in charge of the Army), the then-Department of the Navy, and male-dominated Congress together chose to demobilize women military personnel to the point that they were scarcely visible in the postwar ranks. To make crystal clear their patriarchal point—that a "normal" peacetime military should be a thoroughly masculinized institution—policymakers crafted rules limiting women to a mere 2 percent of the total active-duty force. This was the American military norm throughout the Cold War. The 2 percent limit was kept in place during the Korean and Vietnam wars of the 1950s, 1960s, and early 1970s.

The male leaders of the U.S. Congress, along with their colleagues in the White House and the Defense Department (formerly the War Department and now in charge of all the armed forces, including the newly organized Air Force), did not decide they needed to lift this gendered ceiling until the early 1970s. What changed? Faced with the increasingly unpopular Vietnam War, American policymakers ended

Table 5.1 Percentage of Women in the Active Duty Military, Selected Countries, 2010–2015

Country	% Women	Country	% Women
Australia	12.5	Israel	30.0
Britain	10.0	Japan	5.4
Canada	14.5	Latvia	17.4
China	7.5	New Zealand	16.5
Eritrea	30.0	Russia	10.0
France	15.0	South Africa	26.0
Germany	8.5	United States	14.0

male conscription—what Americans call "the draft"—without changing their vision of the U.S. role in the world, which called for a globally deployed military. That is, they ended the male draft, but held on tightly to their presumed need for thousands of new military recruits every year. This obviously posed a dilemma. Their solution: recruit more women. Still, how to do it in a way that would not surrender the military's long-standing attraction as the place where "boys become men"? How to maintain the military's role in sustaining the country's patriarchal social system? It would become a tricky ideological operation.

The Soviet Union's military planners did much the same. They used thousands of women to help wage their fierce World War II battles against the invading German forces. But at the end of the war, they implemented policies allowing the Soviet military to revert to its "natural" masculinized institutional self, dependent on male conscription. Then, in the 1990s, after the breakup of the Soviet Union, the remaining Russian government launched a draining war against rebel forces in the southern province of Chechnya. Service in the Russian military lost its patriotic appeal. Many Russian mothers even began urging their sons to avoid the draft after these women had uncovered the brutal hazing rituals that drove some young conscripts to commit suicide (Sperling 2003).

In the wake of the failed 1980s war in Afghanistan and as the war in Chechnya dragged on, disillusionment with military service deepened further still. No longer did soldiering seem a rewarding route to authentic manliness. More young male soldiers saw their friends sent home from Afghanistan in sealed zinc coffins or heard from older brothers what awaited them in Chechnya and went absent without leave (AWOL) instead (Alexievich 1992; Eichler 2012). It was at this point that Russian military planners began to look favorably on women as recruits (Mathers 2006). In the late 1990s and early 2000s, the government began recruitment campaigns to persuade women to join the military at the same time as many young Russian women were finding it very difficult to get decent jobs in the uncertain Russian civilian employment market (Cohn 2013).

In neither the United States nor Russia have the male military planners and their legislative colleagues talked about "patriarchy." Those officials and legislators who, after years of deliberately "remasculinizing" their post–World War II militaries, decided to enlist more women volunteers were not motivated chiefly by a desire to liberate women or to lessen masculinized privilege in their country's public life. Instead, both Russian and U.S. officials were motivated primarily by their desire to continue their wide-ranging military operations at a time when they were losing easy access to young male recruits.

South Africa's story is rather different, at least in its most current chapter. The South African government's efforts to enlist women volunteers began in earnest under the country's racist apartheid regime. As the small white ruling minority began to face stronger resistance from the country's combined black, mixed-race, and Asian majority, the country's political leaders, imbued with patriarchal beliefs derived from a strict brand of Calvinist theology, struggled to sustain a large enough military force to match the new challenge to its authoritarian rule: there weren't enough young white male conscripts to fill the ranks. The apartheid regime thus tried to craft a delicate balancing act. They recruited more black South African male volunteers and at the same time—despite the white male elite's very conservative views about respectable femininity—opened new military roles to women volunteers from all communities, though especially white women.

Then in 1994, when the apartheid regime fell and a new constitutional system was created to ensure nonracist democracy, intense discussions began among South Africans about the appropriate composition of the state's newly reconstructed military. There was agreement that this new post-apartheid military should consist wholly of volunteers, not conscripts, and that it should have many more black senior officers. But should it revert to its pre-1980s mostly male composition? South African women's advocates argued that although the just-deposed apartheid elites had recruited large numbers of women into the ranks for the sake of upholding their own racist system, a new democratic military should not simply dismiss women soldiers (Cock 1995). Thus, the fact that today's South African military has one of the world's highest proportions of women in uniform is not the result of a continuation of a recent masculinist and racist political calculation. Rather, it is the product of thoughtful feminist-informed analysis to determine the sorts of relationships between women, the military, and a nascent nonracist political system that would be most likely to ensure a less patriarchal democracy.

Today in dozens of countries an unresolved analytical debate continues over the magnitude—and direction—of military and societal transformation produced by enlisting more women in the military. In 2014, claiming to be acting in the name of gender equality, the Norwegian parliament—much to the surprise and even dismay of many Norwegian feminist peace activists—passed a new law that expanded formerly male-only compulsory military service to women.

Israel is another country in which women's role in the military has become central to debates about not just security, but citizenship. While acknowledging that Israel is one of the very few countries in which both women and men are subject to military conscription, Israeli gender scholars note that women are drafted for shorter terms than men, that most women soldiers are channeled into traditionally feminized military jobs—for instance, secretaries, instructors, nurses, and other adminis- trative positions—and that women are exempted from military service whenever their family responsibilities conflict. In Israeli society, as in most societies, women are seen first and foremost as mothers and daughters, not as architects of the nation's security or as the country's protectors. Most important, it is the male combat soldier who remains the ideal of the true Israeli citizen (Sasson-Levy 2003). Thus, the impressive statistic that 30 percent of the Israeli military are women must be the start, not the end, of a feminist investigation of masculinity, national security, and militarism in Israel—just as such numbers must be the starting points for feminist investigations in other countries.

With that in mind, Israeli feminist investigators have paid close atten- tion to how the Israeli woman soldier is portrayed by the popular Israeli media and by the military establishment itself. Most often, women sol- diers are portrayed as conventionally feminine, sexual, and appealing in the eyes of their male colleagues, as if the woman soldier's physical attractiveness played a role in bolstering the morale of male soldiers, who, the images imply, are the ones actually taking the risks and con- fronting the real dangers in the service of national security (Brownfield- Stein 2006). In any military it is worth monitoring how women soldiers are portrayed in order to chart the ways both the government and ordi- nary citizens try to balance the competing goals of, on the one hand, enlisting women in the country's protective force and, on the other hand, still maintaining many of their own core patriarchal values and beliefs.

An Israeli feminist scholar who explored the same politics of "having their cake and eating it too" listened closely to those women, a minority of a minority, who have been allowed to hold "nontraditional"—that is, presumably masculinized—jobs in the Israeli Defense Forces (IDF). What she found is that these women have done their best to fit into the IDF's dominant masculinized culture. They have often adopted more masculinized humor, more masculinized modes of walking, and lower voice registers. Most of these women in traditionally masculinized jobs have also tried to deny any experiences of sexual harassment by their male colleagues. For instance, one woman soldier, whom the author calls "Rutti," told of noncommissioned officers in her combat-engineering platoon taunting her with "Rutti is a whore." She never thought of reporting incidents like this. Instead, Rutti tried to shrug it off, saying, "Obviously, it wasn't fun. It's annoying, but you can't take it too hard. It's a trivial song, nobody notices it, nobody pays attention to it" (Sasson-Levy, 2003). While such a personal interpretation may work as a private survival strategy for a woman isolated in a masculinized institution, letting such misogynistic and harassing practices go unchallenged leaves the existing masculinized military culture firmly in place, perhaps even reaffirmed (Sasson-Levy 2003).

A current international debate is over this question: Would UN peacekeeping missions be more effective in war zones if the contributing states' military contingents (the "blue helmets") had higher proportions of women soldiers?

The responsibility for contributing troops to UN global peacekeeping missions is not shared equally. A majority of these blue-helmeted soldiers come from poor countries. Among the top contributors today are Nepal, Uruguay, Benin, Cameroon, Senegal, Rwanda, Niger, Burundi, and Indonesia.

In 2015, a mere 3 percent of military personnel deployed on UN peacekeeping operations around the world were women. Men constituted 97 percent of those soldiers contributed by member states to UN peacekeeping missions. At the same time, men made up 90 percent of all the police personnel contributed to UN peacekeeping missions to conflict areas; only 10 percent were women (www.un.org/en/peacekeeping).

The proponents of increasing the presence of women soldiers and police officers in globalized peace operations argue that women do not spark local antagonisms as much as male soldiers do. One male officer responsible for training Indian army officers for peacekeeping assignments said that women officers were valuable for "their ability to pick up local languages . . . [and for] their knack for integrating their own culture with new ones" (*Hindustan Times* 2006). They also, this line of reasoning continues, are more able to create meaningful relationships with local women, crucial players in reweaving social fabrics after war. Some proponents of increasing the proportions of women soldiers in international peacekeeping deployments draw on essentialist understandings of gender, arguing that women are by nature better at peacebuilding than are men.

Yet some feminist peace activists, for instance those in New Zealand, have voiced concern that some government officials will imagine that simply adding more women soldiers to their own UN peacekeeping contingents will be a sufficient action to roll back patriarchal approaches to international peacebuilding. These analysts insist that meaningful peacebuilding will require a lot deeper gendered transformation (Peace Movement Aotearoa, 2015).

When government officials—legislators, defense experts, military planners—consider a wide range of questions when they devise military recruitment strategies, typically they deny asking some of these:

- Who is trustworthy enough to be given a gun?
- Whose exclusion from the new security forces will undermine the fragile peace?
- Whose exclusion won't matter?
- Whose inclusion in the ranks will make the new military trusted by the general citizenry?
- Whose skills are needed?
- Whose immediate needs are best satisfied via the pay and other rewards and benefits that soldiering brings?

Typically, these discussions feature debates about ethnic, regional, racial, class, and political party loyalties—not gender. The unspoken presumption shared by the participants around the policymaking table—that is, the local leaders and overseas donors, advisors, and diplomats—frequently is that they are talking about men. Why? Because it is widely believed that it is men's rivalries and unmet needs that will upset the tenuous calm. It is the threats that men pose that must be urgently addressed. And only occasionally is the exclusion of women from the ranks and officer corps of the new military deemed a threat to the fragile postwar peace. Women? Their issues can wait until later. But "later" can be a long time away.

Sometimes, however, the topic of women's inclusion does get on the table, especially if some of the people around the table have broader, less-militarized notions of "national security." These people (some perhaps with personal experience in women's grassroots groups) will likely be thinking of dismantling the masculinist culture of the former military, perhaps seeing masculinist military culture—and not simply past ethnic or partisan loyalties—as at least partly to blame for outbreaks of violence and as sowing the seeds of civilian distrust and alienation. Still, underneath the surface of the discussion will lurk the nagging question: does adding more women to a military have any significant impact at all?

Since the 1980s, some Japanese defense policymakers have adopted a similar mode of thinking. On the one hand, Japan has a constitution that pledges the country both to never again adopt military force as a means of resolving problems and to refrain from creating a military with which to wield such force. On the other hand, today Japan (thanks in part to the strong urging of the U.S. government) actually has a formidable military equipped with the most up-to-date technology. In practice, the Japanese military, whose formal name is the Japan Self-Defense Forces (SDF), deploys its soldiers only on humanitarian missions, and the soldiers never fire their guns.

Yet there is a profound awkwardness that the Japanese must cope with: the fact that the constitutional antimilitary principle exists side by side with an institutional reality. One way male policymakers have devised for smoothing out the contradictions that are creating this sense of this political unease is to bring more Japanese women into the SDF. Women constitute only 5 percent of total SDF personnel today, and their roles do not give them much influence in military decision-making. But male policymakers hope that putting the nonthreatening smiling faces of young SDF women on the military's recruitment ads and other public relations materials will reassure Japanese supporters of the country's post–World War II nonaggression principles that the SDF is a friendly, nonviolent institution. For some of the young women soldiers themselves who enlisted with hopes of avoiding the tokenism they routinely encounter in Japanese civilian companies, this superficial public relations ploy generates not pride, but disappointment and frustration (Frühstück 2006).

This Japanese debate over military recruitment has taken on new salience with the governing party, the Liberal Democratic Party, being led by a prime minster determined to remilitarize Japan. Shinzo Abe sees Japan's current "peace constitution" as a drag on Japan's global influence. His argument is that Japan will only be treated by other international elites as a "mature" player in the global community (for instance, gaining a seat as a permanent member of the UN Security Council) if it expands its military's role in international affairs. Many Japanese disagree. Among the most outspoken opponents of this vision are Japanese feminists.

Optimistic commentators on military affairs predict that increasing the proportion of women (thus decreasing the proportion of men) in a military will make that military less patriarchal: the higher the percentage of women in a military, they believe, the less the traditional privileging of masculinity will be able to survive. Patriarchal beliefs and ways of relating simply will prove untenable.

If they are dedicated optimists, they might go further and even predict that this military will become less militarized. Yes, a less-militarized military. What would that look like? Sandra Whitworth, a Canadian feminist and international politics expert, has been critical of how militarized the Canadian UN peacekeeping operations have become. Still, she starts off her thoughtful book about militarized peacekeeping with a tribute to a seemingly less-militarized military: she candidly recalls how glad she was to see Canadian soldiers arrive at her farmhouse in the midst of a brutal ice storm. They were soldiers, but they were also friendly, helpful, nonviolent rescuers (Whitworth 2004).

During the years 2006–2015, under the leadership of Prime Minister Stephen Harper and his Conservative government, the Canadian military became more militarized as it followed the US-led NATO operations into Afghanistan. After Justin Trudeau and his Liberal Party won a new majority in the 2015 Canadian parliamentary elections, however, the process was reversed. One of his first acts as the new prime minister was to end the Canadian military's combat role in Afghanistan, a step that might have signaled a more general demilitarization the country's foreign policy. It will take a gender analyst, though, to investigate whether this change alters the relationships of masculinities and femininities inside the Canadian military.

A less-militarized military would be one less focused on a combat role and less imbued with an institutional culture of masculinized violence. It would be a military less committed to a hierarchical, threat-filled worldview; having an "enemy" wouldn't be so central to the military's raison d'être. It would also be a military whose soldiers and their senior officers would take at least as much (or more?) satisfaction in rescuing civilians from the ravages of ice storms, hurricanes, and earthquakes as in rolling into a combat zone in their intimidating armored vehicles. It would be a military in which officers who serve in successful humanitarian operations, not those with combat experience, would have the best chance of being promoted to general or admiral.

According to this optimistic analysis, if, for instance, the proportion of women soldiers rises from just 1 percent of the state's military to 15 percent, masculinization and patriarchy—as well as militarization—will likely be stalled and perhaps even rolled back.

Of course, there is a second, less rosy forecast: increasing the percentage of women serving inside the state's military could cause those women to become more militarized. Simultaneously, pessimists predict, the general public's acceptance of women as soldiers will send the roots of militarizing culture down even deeper into the ecology of the entire society. A military with at least 10 percent women in its ranks will no longer look "out of step" with the rest of society. That is, with at least a smattering of women (and featuring those women in recruiting ads, as well as encouraging media coverage of their activities) a military won't look like a bastion of bygone maleness. The military thereby will be harder than ever to distinguish from civilian society. That could make it harder to scrutinize the military's persistent masculinized institutional culture and to raise questions about the military's exemptions from many of the rules and procedures that the civilian public must live by. This more pessimistic analytical forecast is based on the assessment that masculinization, militarization, and patriarchy don't just roll over in the face of change. Each operates within the military as a socializing pressure: the "outsiders" (women) entering the military's realm are likely to adopt as their own the already established—and rewarding—patriarchal beliefs and values.

There is yet a third possibility. Sustaining and challenging patriarchy—these opposing forces might coexist in the same society, or in the same institution. Thus, so too might militarizing and demilitarizing processes. The result would be a surprising mix of pressures and tendencies. An important characteristic of militarized patriarchal states and patriarchal militaries: their policymakers can be confused, contradictory, and ambivalent.

Those men and women who have a stake in perpetuating a patriarchal culture and structure—who see it as good for themselves, good for their families, good for their own society, and even good for the world—are not immune to confusion. For instance, they may want to preserve the dominant masculine culture of their state's military and, at the same time, conclude that it is necessary to enlist more women because birthrates are dropping (and so the pool of young men is shrinking), because more male conscripts are going AWOL, or because nervous legislators are responding to the public's disillusionment by voting to end male conscription. Trying to achieve both of these goals can produce confusion and contradictory actions.

The temptation among patriarchal policymakers, however, is to deny confusion—to hide it, to camouflage it under a paint job of convoluted justification. Usually this compels those confused policymakers to spend a lot of energy trying to manipulate definitions of "femininity." In doing this, they will probably look like the South Korean regime of Chung Hee Park, which in the 1960s and 1970s mobilized young women to leave home in order to serve as "cheap labor" in sneaker and electronics factories, while it simultaneously tried to convince these young women and their parents that "dutiful daughter" was their chief feminine identity.

Any patriarchy survives and thrives only if its leaders and members can perpetuate a widely accepted standard of "proper" femininity. A dominant notion of "proper" femininity is especially potent when it becomes the basis by which women (and girls) judge, or "police," each other. Such daily judging—of girls and women by girls and women—creates divisive hierarchies among women, making it more likely that they will see other girls or women as sources of competition or even as threats to their own sense of well-being. This sort of preoccupation makes it less likely that girls and women will notice how the larger pattern of relationships, rules, and presumptions of patriarchy shapes their own lives, much less that they will join together as women to challenge masculinized privilege. That is, when racism, class prejudice, nationalism, patriotism, militarism, and competition for boyfriends and husbands divide women and girls and divert their attention, patriarchy becomes more secure.

Second, if the promoters of a patriarchal system are skillful, they will manage to make "femininity" appear natural—not the product of human decisions. This feat makes their own uses of power harder to see. If they can achieve this, then the entire patriarchal order is likely to take on the status of "natural" and thus not open to fundamental challenge.

Yet as we can see when we pay close attention to women in the military, there are many times when promoters of patriarchy find it difficult to sustain the naturalness of the dichotomy between "masculinity" and "femininity" and the propriety (positive value) of a certain mode of feminine behavior. These times of patriarchal discomfort and confusion are especially useful to explore. That exploration is likely to bear the most fruit if one conducts it with an explicit feminist curiosity, because a feminist curiosity will keep one alert to how even confused ideas about masculinity and femininity can determine who has power and who is marginalized.

Patriarchal confusion often occurs during wartime or when a government is most eager to prepare for war. At first glance, this may seem unlikely. After all, it is during wartime that the masculinity of the protector is most entrenched in its privilege, while the dependent femininity of the grateful protected is most celebrated. But let's look again. And listen. Researchers who have been digging into the complex realities of the American Civil War, World War II, the Vietnam War, and the current wars in Africa and the Middle East are showing us that policymakers who believe in the naturalness and rightness of a patriarchal social order nonetheless will violate conventional tenets of masculine and feminine difference so that they can use women in new, "nontraditional" ways for the sake of bolstering their war-waging efforts.

It is not that these wartime patriarchal officials have shed their patriarchal beliefs and values. Instead, feminist historians have revealed, these officials convince themselves that they can violate their own (and most civilians') gender rules just for the war years and then, in peacetime, reestablish the alleged "natural order." In practice, this turns out to be politically risky because it can produce confusion.

As intriguing as it is to explore this militarized patriarchal confusion, some feminist investigators have been wary of devoting intellectual energy to the study of women who become soldiers. These investigators worry that simply by taking seriously the condition of women in the military and such women's experiences and ideas, they unintentionally might help legitimize both the military as a public institution and soldiering as an occupation. The worries of these feminists are rooted in a smart, if pessimistic, analysis that recognizes how seductive militarization can be. It is true that a researcher or journalist (feminist or nonfeminist) can start out neutrally studying a military and can then gradually—unconsciously—start absorbing not only the discourse but the deeper assumptions of that military and of its civilian strategists (Cohn 1987).

However, the militarization of a researcher (or journalist) is not inevitable (Basham, Belkin, and Gifkins 2015; Enloe 2015). To do feminist research of any patriarchal institution and of women living their lives inside that patriarchal institution (e.g., women in corporations, women in legislatures, women in civil service, women in law firms) one does need to acknowledge the risks and thus to cultivate a heightened consciousness of how one's own compassion and imagination, one's own sense of the "good story," one's own sense of "seriousness" each can become militarized in the process of investigating women inside militaries. The telltale sign that one's investigation of women inside militaries is becoming militarized may be that one stops asking about militarism. One begins to be interested solely in equality and inequality. However, the risks and the effort it takes to avoid those risks are worth taking, for we will never fully understand patriarchy's adaptive qualities and its limits if we avoid studying those women who are trying to pursue their own goals inside such patriarchal institutions.

The importance of this gendered assignment strategy means that one should always keep a sharp eye on any military's changing definitions of combat. For instance, even within NATO, whose leaders put so much emphasis on the standardization of weaponry and doctrine, there have been definitional differences in what constitutes a "combat" job and thus where women can or cannot serve alongside men. Moreover, some NATO members have gone further: since the late 1980s, some have eliminated the male-only combat rule altogether. The Dutch led the way, followed closely by the Norwegians and the Canadians.

The Americans and British were among the most reluctant to give up the male-only combat rule. Thus, it is they who continued to invest the most political energy in defining and redefining exactly what constitutes "combat." In the 1980s, for instance, the U.S. Army broadened the definition of "combat" to include even the jobs done by electricians and carpenters because, allegedly, carpenters and electricians sometimes were called upon to perform their work near the line of fire. This meant that women soldiers could be excluded from jobs as electricians and carpenters in the name of protecting them from the dangers of combat. One of the facts that made the male-only combat rule seem irrational was that all thirteen of the U.S. military women who were killed in the Gulf War of 1990–1991 were women in what were bureaucratically then defined as "noncombat" positions (Enloe 1993, 2000).

During the next decade, under pressure from the Women's Caucus in Congress—and facing the need to have more flexibility in assignments—the army narrowed its definition of "combat." Only in 2013 did the U.S. government, under President Barack Obama, with Congressional support, drop its ban on women in combat. On the other hand, actual implementation proved far more murky, with each branch of the armed services crafting their own measures to position women in combat—or to keep them out (Mackenzie 2015).

In most of today's modernized militaries, it is the submarine corps, armored divisions, fighter plane squadrons, paratroops, infantry regiments, and irregular elite forces, such as the U.S. Army's Special Forces, that remain the inner sanctums of masculinity. Perhaps not surprisingly, these are also the groups within most militaries that are the principal recruiting grounds for future generals and admirals. This is how patriarchy operates in an era of women's rights and globalized modernization.

Under pressure from citizens, many governments have ended male conscription. These are the governments that have been the most determined to enlist more women as volunteers without sacrificing their military's useful masculinized culture. These governments' military strategists have become especially interested in recruiting those young women with high school or even college educations because modern militaries rely on higher literacy and mathematical skills, and in many countries today a higher proportion of young women than young men are completing high school and college.

On the other hand, officials do not want women's presence in their military to dilute what they see to be the essence of the institution: its deep affiliation with manliness. So, at the same time as they recruit women to acquire their needed skills, these officials worry that if the military's core masculinized culture is significantly diluted, two dire things will happen. First, a weakened masculinized esprit de corps will produce a military that is a less-effective instrument of coercive force. Second, if the popular image of soldiering loses its masculine aura, a lot of young men (potential enlistees) will decide to walk right past the recruiter's office: "Who wants to join an organization that's gone the way of bank telling?" It is with these two patriarchal anxieties (about military effectiveness and about male psychology) in their minds that most military planners and their civilian colleagues go about trying to craft their strategies for recruiting and deploying women to compensate for the men they have lost with the end of male conscription. It has turned out to be a "patriarchal challenge." The resulting practices, not surprisingly, have been confusing, contradictory, and often harmful to the women recruits.

Military policymakers have become more reliant on women recruits, yet still seek to reassure the public (and male soldiers) that men in the military will not surrender their "masculinity" when serving with women and that even women who join the military will stay "feminine." Such an insistent reassurance might imply to some listeners that one can masculinize or demasculinize any activity. Yes, a soldier in khaki sitting in an office at a typewriter pecking out the commander's memos might have been secure in his masculinity back in the 1940s, but in the 2000s that is a military job that should be done by a khaki-clad woman. The implication: the differences between women and men are not so intrinsically natural after all. Instead, the differences between what men do and what women do are largely the product of human imagination and decision-making. At this point, the patriarchal alarm bells might begin to ring.

> Dear Worried Patriarchal Public,
>
> We are bringing women into this military institution, where you and we know they do not naturally belong, for the sake of national security. National security must take priority over our beliefs about what is natural and what is proper. But don't worry. We know this is a temporary aberration. We, like you, know this is not natural; it is not what we are all fighting for. So we guarantee you that we will rely on this aberration for only a brief time, until we win this war. Then, dear public, having won the war, we will return women to their domestic spheres where they really

*belong and so the military back to its natural masculinized order and thus
the whole social order back to normal. Trust us.*

This is an imagined letter to confused citizens from military planners
struggling to cope with personnel shortages. The patriarchal message is:
once the war is over, once the threat to national security has receded,
then the natural and proper gendered social order will be reassuringly
restored. This implicit message—sent out in various forms by governments as diverse as the Soviet government, the American government,
and the South African government—makes the postwar years a time to
watch carefully. For the reassuring implication is that in the postwar era,
women will return—or be returned—to their natural and proper feminine places and roles. Even in revolutionary Algeria, China, Guatemala,
Vietnam, El Salvador, and Eritrea, these patterns have indeed been
repeated: once the imminent threat to national security has receded,
women's public space shrinks. Most obvious is the demobilization of
women from the ranks of the military. But this demobilization often goes
hand in hand with the remasculinization of other spheres of public life
such as political parties, factory work, and farm management (Krosch
2005; Turner 1998).

Therefore, as investigators, we need to turn our feminist curiosity
to the weeks, months, and even years immediately following the formal end of any inter-state or civil war. Those will be the times when—
blatantly or subtly—policymakers (and their allies in the media,
academia, and business) will try to take steps to terminate the wartime
"aberration" and return the military (and thus society) to its patriarchal "normality."

That is, to make sense of the gendered dynamics of homegrown and
globalized militarization, the postwar years are as interesting to investigate as the war years.

CHAPTER 6

WIELDING MASCULINITY INSIDE ABU GHRAIB AND GUANTÁNAMO

In June 2006, two years after the Abu Ghraib scandal broke and set off worldwide outrage, a short article appeared in the *New York Times* reporting that an American army dog handler had been found guilty by a military court-martial. He had been charged with having used his dog to intimidate Iraqi male prisoners being held by the U.S. military at Abu Ghraib (Associated Press 2006), an infamous military jail and interrogation center in Iraq. Sergeant Santos A. Cardona was the eleventh American soldier serving there to have been convicted of violations of the U.S. military code of conduct. His defense lawyers had argued, unsuccessfully, that Sergeant Cardona was doing only what he had been trained to do and what his military superiors had commanded him to do.

Three of the eleven American soldiers convicted of committing abuses at Abu Ghraib were women, eight were men. All eleven soldiers who were court-martialed and convicted were enlisted personnel or noncommissioned officers. None were higher-ranking officers. None were Washington-based civilian policymakers (Hillman 2005).

The only senior officer to receive an official reprimand and demotion was a woman, General Janis Karpinski. She was the army reserve officer then in charge of the U.S. occupation authority's cobbled-together military prison system in Iraq. Her own telling of the Abu Ghraib story is full of descriptions of wartime unpreparedness, lack of senior command support, autonomous actions by military and CIA interrogators, and routine behaviors in what has become the military's institutional culture of sexism (Karpinski 2005).

On the same June day in 2006 that the *New York Times* reported Sergeant Cardona's conviction, the paper's editors included two other reports that one could read as possibly connected to the short article about Abu Ghraib. First, there was another brief report of the last of the U.S. Army's trials concerning abuses at a U.S. detention center at the Bagram military base in Afghanistan. The last soldier to be prosecuted for abuse and the deaths of prisoners held at Bagram was Private First Class Damien M. Corsetti. He was one of more than a dozen U.S. soldiers—all men—charged with abusing and causing the deaths of Afghan prisoners at Bagram. The military jury acquitted Private Corsetti (Golden 2006).

Since the U.S. government pulled out most of its soldiers from Iraq, American memories of the U.S.-led war there have begun to fade. Students now in university were in elementary school when the Abu Ghraib revelations broke in the press and on social media. Today, most of those found guilty of misconduct at the U.S.-run prison have completed their prison terms. The senior executive, military, and CIA officials responsible for the prison and the interrogations have gone on to other posts or have retired from office. The prison itself is now under the management of the Iraqi government. The several serious investigations into the uses of torture by contemporary governments attracted brief public attention, but today are gathering dust on many bookshelves (Senate Select Committee on Intelligence, 2014).

Nonetheless, there are lessons to be learned from the American actions at Abu Ghraib and the American responses to those actions, lessons still imperative to learn now. Among those lessons for today is: *Using gender analysis will expose the workings of militarized power that otherwise will be missed.*

The Geneva Conventions are international agreements negotiated by governments in the mid-twentieth century. The agreements are not designed so much to reverse militarization as they are intended to globalize the ethics that should guide governments' war-waging behavior. War waging can continue but should be conducted according to these agreed-upon rules. The U.S. government is a signatory to the Geneva Conventions. Prescriptions for the treatment of prisoners captured in wartime is one of the major elements of the Geneva Conventions. That is, a soldier may be in the enemy's forces, but he or she is still a human being and, as a human being, deserves to be treated humanely.

Avoiding these internationally agreed-upon requirements to treat prisoners of war humanely was a strategy adopted by U.S. government officials in the name of

- "urgency," coupled with
- "national security," in order to wage
- "the global war on terror."

Those who devised the political rationales, legal interpretations, and bureaucratic strategies for this avoidance were overwhelmingly civilians. They were civilians during the administration of George W. Bush who were posted inside the Defense Department, the Justice Department, the White House legal counsel's office, and the office of the vice president (Danner 2004; Mayer 2005a; Mayer 2005b; Mayer 2005c; Mayer 2006).

Witnesses for both the defense and the prosecution at the June 2006 Corsetti court-martial described how the pressures imposed on guards and interrogators at Bagram to get more information from their prisoners increased in late 2002. It was then two months into the U.S.-led military invasion of Afghanistan. President Bush had declared that prisoners captured in Afghanistan were not to be deemed eligible for the international protections guaranteed to enemy combatants under the Geneva Conventions. Many of those male prisoners first detained and questioned at Bagram would soon be flown in large cargo planes—after they had been dressed in orange jump suits, shackled, and had burlap bags placed over their heads—to the detention center the United States had recently constructed at its naval base in Guantánamo, Cuba (Lipman 2009). The links between Bagram and Guantánamo were being forged.

A year later, those forged links would be extended to Abu Ghraib. Trying to make sense of what happened inside Abu Ghraib in the fall and winter of 2003 turns out to be nearly impossible if one treats Abu Ghraib as an island. It was not an island. It was a link in a globalized chain (Greenberg and Dratel 2005) of prisons. Among the materials used to weld those chain links—Bagram to Guantánamo, Guantánamo to Abu Ghraib—were American ideas about feminization.

Feminization is a process of imposing allegedly feminine characteristics on a person—man or woman—or a group or a kind of activity. Often the goal of feminizing someone (or something) is to lower his (or its) status. Feminization provokes anxiety when particular forms of masculinity are culturally, academically, politically, or economically privileged (Carver 2003; Elias 2009). Stitching sneakers for the global market has been feminized in the corporate hope of lowering labor costs. Military nursing has been feminized in an effort to use women in the military without diluting the military's prized image as a masculinized institution. A male candidate running for election against another male candidate may try to gain an advantage with voters by feminizing his opponent—for instance, by portraying his rival as "weak on national security." A male prisoner is feminized when his captors force him to look or act in ways those captors think will make him feel feminine. The presumption motivating his taunters is that a man who is being feminized will become more cooperative out of his sense of shame and helplessness.

In a patriarchal global culture—in rich countries and poor countries, in countries of diverse cultural traditions—any person, group, or activity that can be feminized risks losing his or her (or its) influence, authority, and even self-respect. So long as any culture remains patriarchal, then, feminization can be wielded as an instrument of intimidation.

Using a feminist curiosity to make sense of what happened in Abu Ghraib requires (a) investigating any efforts to wield feminization in imprisonment and interrogation and (b) looking for the women in all their various roles. Those roles can be both obvious and obscure.

Ann Wright served as an army officer for twenty-nine years and then as a U.S. diplomat before resigning in opposition to the administration's preemptive war. After resigning, Ann Wright decided to use her new independence to find out where all the women were on the broad canvas that became "Abu Ghraib." She found Major General Barbara Fast, chief of military intelligence, serving in the U.S. military command's head-quarters in Baghdad. She found Captain Carolyn Wood, a military intelligence officer who had been the leader of the interrogation team in Bagram and then, with her unit, transferred to Abu Ghraib. Wright found two lower-ranking women interrogators deployed to Abu Ghraib, as well as two women employed as interpreters by a civilian contractor, the Titan Company, working with a military intelligence unit inside the prison. Ann Wright also found three Army linguists working in inter-rogation teams at Guantánamo during 2003 and 2004. She discovered that during these same crucial months at least three other Army women were conducting interrogations at Guantánamo. An unknown number of additional women were serving at Guantánamo at the same time as private contract interrogators. None of these women came forward to stop the abuses they witnessed. Several of them, according to firsthand accounts, helped devise some of the practices meant to humiliate the male prisoners (Saar 2005; Wright 2006).

Is it surprising that in 2003 and 2004 there were so many American women inside Bagram, Guantánamo, and Abu Ghraib who, were play-ing roles up and down the chain of command as guards, interpreters, and interrogators? Probably not. After all, over the past two decades, in devising gender strategies for recruiting women while still maintaining the military's masculinized core—combat—officials of the U.S. Defense Department had channeled women soldiers into not just nursing and administration but such seemingly noncontroversial jobs as military police, military interpreters, and intelligence. By 2004, women, who made up only 15 percent of total U.S. Army personnel, represented 22 percent of military police and 25 percent of military interrogators (Wright 2006).

Still, doing a gender analysis fueled by feminist curiosity to investigate Abu Ghraib, Bagram, and Guantánamo allows one to do more than find where the women are—as revealing as that exploration is. Using a femi-nist curiosity prompts one to also pursue the answer to a question that most commentators fail to ask: What are the causes and consequences of wielding ideas about masculinity and femininity?

Feminization was used during the 2001–2010 Afghanistan and Iraq wars mainly by American militarized men (civilian and military), but with the complicity and sometimes the direct involvement of a handful of American militarized women. Evidence suggests that feminization was intended by its wartime wielders to humiliate and thereby gain information from foreign men, mostly men identified by their American captors as "Muslim," "dangerous," and "the enemy." As they were transported by U.S. officials from Washington to Bagram to Guantánamo to Abu Ghraib, these practices of coercive feminization might be thought of as being globally militarized.

Back at Private Corsetti's June 2006 (scarcely reported) court-martial, defense witnesses sought to undercut the prosecution's case against Corsetti by noting that there were almost-daily phone calls to interrogators at Bagram from their American civilian Defense Department superiors in Washington. Their Washington-based superiors were infused with a sense of urgency. They demanded quick results from the interrogations being conducted at the Bagram base. The witnesses recalled how this pressure from Washington officials served to increase the aggressiveness of the physical tactics that Bagram soldiers and interrogators used on prisoners deemed uncooperative (Golden 2006). Members of the jury seemed convinced.

American military interrogators' and guards' adoption of both painful "stress positions" and feminization to intimidate captive men can be traded globally, just as rifles can be traded globally, just as ideas about national security and creating "cheap labor" can be traded globally.

American male and female soldiers serving during late 2003 and early 2004 as prison guards in Abu Ghraib became the best-known actors in this fast-globalizing drama. As individuals, they seemed far from being global players. They appeared quite parochial and isolated. The photographs that showed them deliberately humiliating and torturing scores of Iraqi men held in detention and under interrogation were taken by those soldiers apparently for their own private amusement, not for prime-time television or headline stories. But their audience expanded beyond their wildest dreams—or nightmares. Between April and June 2004, millions of viewers were looking at these private photos: American soldiers smiling broadly as they appeared to be taking enormous pleasure in frightening and humiliating their wartime Iraqi charges.

Most people who saw these photographs can still describe the scenes. An American male soldier standing in a self-satisfied pose, facing his army colleague holding the camera with his arms crossed and wearing surgical blue rubber gloves, a sign that this abuse was occurring in the age of AIDS. In front of him, we, the globalized viewers of these photographs, could see an American woman soldier smiling at the camera as she leaned on top of a pile of naked Iraqi men who were being forced to contort themselves into a human pyramid.

Other pictures whizzed around the planet via social media. An American woman soldier, again smiling, holding an Iraqi male prisoner on a leash. An American woman soldier pointing to a naked Iraqi man's genitals, apparently treating them as a joke. American male soldiers intimidating naked Iraqi male prisoners with snarling guard dogs. An Iraqi male prisoner standing alone on a box, his head covered with a hood and electrical wires attached to different parts of his body. An Iraqi male prisoner forced to wear women's underwear. Not pictured, but substantiated, were Iraqi men forced to masturbate and to simulate oral sex with each other, as well as an Iraqi woman prisoner coerced by several American male soldiers into kissing them (Hersh 2004).

Few of the U.S. government's official investigators or the mainstream news commentators used feminist insights to make sense of what went on in the prison (Danner 2004; Strasser 2004). The result is that we have not really gotten to the bottom of the Abu Ghraib story. This failure, I think, could undercut our collective attempts to understand how militarization can lead to torture.

This omission of a feminist analysis in investigations of Abu Ghraib—and of abusive actions inside Bagram and Guantánamo, as well as the connections forged between these places—could also limit our attempts to implement those changes that can enforce globalized treaties and conventions intended to either roll back militarization or at least reduce its harmful effects.

One place to start employing a feminist set of tools is to explain why one American woman soldier in particular—not even a guard, just a low-ranking clerk visiting the cell block the night the photos were taken—captured the attention of so many media editors and ordinary viewers and readers: the then twenty-one-year-old enlisted army reservist Lynndie England. Today England is a civilian, a former convict (completing her eventual three-year military prison sentence in 2008), a single mother (of a child fathered by army colleague Charles Graner), living with her parents in West Virginia, doing volunteer work and earning a modest income as a part-time secretary (http://worldnews .nbcnews.com/_news/2013/03/19/17373769-iraq-war-10-years-later).

Why didn't the name of Charles Graner, the apparent cell-block ringleader of the photographed abuses become as well known as England? More important: Why didn't the name of General Geoffrey Miller become globally known? General Geoffrey Miller was the commander of Guantánamo and, when he was sent to Iraq, became the carrier of Washington's message from Guantánamo to Abu Ghraib—a message that this was a time demanding a sense of urgency, an urgency that called for more aggressive techniques in interrogations of Iraqi prisoners held in Abu Ghraib (Hersh 2004). The fact that neither Graner's nor, especially, Miller's name did become as familiar reflects the gendering not just of the abuse but also of the political consciousnesses of ordinary Americans and news consumers around the world: women in presumably masculinized places, such as a military prison in a war zone, make a better "story."

Several things proved shocking to the millions of viewers of the clandestine prison photos. First, the Abu Ghraib scenes suggested there existed a gaping chasm between, on the one hand, the Bush administration's claim that its military invasion and overthrow of the brutal Saddam Hussein regime would bring a civilizing sort of "freedom" to the Iraqi people and, on the other hand, the seemingly barbaric treatment that American soldiers were willfully meting out to Iraqis held in captivity without trial. Second, it was shocking to witness such blatant abuse of imprisoned detainees by soldiers representing a government that had passed its own anti-torture laws and had signed both the international Geneva Conventions against mistreatment of wartime combatants and the UN Convention against Torture and Other Cruel, Inhuman or Degrading Treatment or Punishment (sometimes referred to simply as the "Convention Against Torture").

Yet there was a third source of shock that prompted scores of early media commentaries and intense conversations among ordinary viewers: seeing women engage in torture. Of the seven American soldiers initially court-martialed (and eleven soldiers eventually court-martialed), all low-ranking army reserve military police guards, three were women. Somehow, the American male soldier in the blue surgical gloves (Charles Graner) was not shocking to most viewers and so did not inspire much private consternation or a stream of op-ed columns. Women, by contrast, were conventionally expected by most editors and news watchers to appear in wartime as mothers and wives of soldiers, occasionally as military nurses and truck mechanics, and most often as victims of wartime violence. Women were not—according to the conventional presumption—supposed to be the wielders of violence and certainly not the perpetrators of torture. When those deeply gendered presumptions were turned upside down, many people felt a sense of shock. "This is awful; how could this have happened?"

Private First Class Lynndie England, the young female military clerk (not a guard) photographed holding the man on a leash, thus became the source of intense public curiosity. The news photographers could not restrain themselves two months later, in early August 2004, from showing England in her camouflaged army maternity uniform when she appeared at Fort Bragg for her pretrial hearing. She had become pregnant as a result of her sexual liaison with another enlisted reservist while on duty in Abu Ghraib. Her sexual partner was Charles Graner. Yet Charles Graner's name was scarcely mentioned. He apparently was doing what men are expected to do in wartime: have sex and wield violence. The public's curiosity and its lack of curiosity thus matched its pattern of shock. All three—curiosity, lack of curiosity, and shock—were conventionally gendered. Using a feminist investigatory approach, one should find this lack of public and media curiosity about Charles Graner just as revealing as the public's and media's fascination with Lynndie England.

Yet more than just Charles Graner was pushed aside. The government policymaking that implicitly approved the use of torture was never put on trial. In fact, one reporter who, with a handful of her colleagues followed the Abu Ghraib trials for months, all the way through to the trial of Lynndie England (the last of the eleven low-ranking Abu Ghraib soldiers to be tried) and heard Lynndie England's sentence pronounced in the courtroom at Fort Hood, Texas, in September 2005, noted how narrow the focus remained throughout all the trials. Bigger issues were deemed irrelevant (Wypijewski 2006). In fact, it was considered quite exceptional when General Geoffrey Miller, the Guantánamo commander who had brought the message to Iraq in the fall of 2003 that pressure on captured suspected insurgents needed to be increased, appeared briefly at just one of the many court sessions. No senior civilian officials from the Defense or Justice departments made any appearances. This legalistic narrowing of the focus served to normalize in the minds of many ordinary people those government interrogation policies and the resultant practice of inflicting physical pain and feminized humiliation that flowed from them.

Responding to the torrent of Abu Ghraib stories coming out of Iraq during the spring and summer of 2004, President George W. Bush and Secretary of Defense Donald Rumsfeld, the president's appointee, tried to reassure the public that the abusive behavior inside the prison was not representative of America, nor did it reflect the Bush administration's own foreign policies. Rather, the Abu Ghraib abuses were the work of "rogue" soldiers, a "few bad apples."

The "bad apple" explanation always goes like this: the institution is working fine, its values are appropriate, its internal dynamics sustain positive values, along with respectful, productive behavior. Thus, according to the "bad apple" explanation, nothing needs to be reassessed or reformed in the way the organization works; all that needs to happen to stop the abuse is to prosecute and remove those few individuals who refused to play by the established rules. Sometimes this may be true. Some listeners to the Bush administration's "bad apple" explanation, however, weren't reassured. They wondered if the Abu Ghraib abuses were not produced by just a few bad apples found in a solid, reliable barrel but instead were produced by an essentially "bad barrel." They also wondered whether this "barrel" embraced not only the Abu Ghraib prison, but the larger interlocking U.S. military, intelligence, and civilian command structures (Hersh 2004; Human Rights Watch 2004).

What makes a "barrel" go bad? That is, what turns an organization, an institution, or a whole system into one that ignores, perhaps even fosters, abusive behavior by the individuals operating inside it? This question is relevant for every workplace, every political system, every international alliance. Here, too, feminists have been working hard over the past three decades to develop a curiosity and a set of analytical tools with which we can all answer this important question. So many of us today live much of our lives within complex organizations, large and small—workplaces, local and national governments, health care systems, criminal justice systems, international organizations. Feminist researchers have revealed that virtually all organizations are gendered; that is, all organizations are shaped by the ideas about, and daily practices of wielding, norms of masculinity and femininity (Bunster-Burotto 1985; Burke 2004; Ehrenreich 2004; Enloe 2013; Whitworth 2004).

Ignoring the workings of gender, as feminist investigators have found, makes it impossible for us to explain accurately what makes any organization "tick." That failure makes it impossible for us to hold an organization accountable.

Yet most of the long official reports on the Abu Ghraib abuse scandal were written by people who ignored these feminist organizational lessons. They acted as if the dynamics of masculinity and femininity among low-level guards and high-level policymakers made no difference. Relying on such an assumption is very risky.

A series of U.S. Senate hearings, along with several Defense Department investigations, tried to explain what went wrong in Abu Ghraib and why. The most authoritative of the Defense Department reports were the "Taguba Report," the "Fay/Jones Report" (both named after generals who headed these investigations), and the "Schlesinger Report" (named after a civilian former secretary of defense who chaired this investigatory team) (Human Rights Watch 2004; Jehl 2004; Lewis and Schmitt 2004; Schmitt 2004; Taguba 2004). In addition, the CIA conducted its own investigation, since its officials were deeply involved in interrogating—and often hiding in secret prisons—captured Afghans and Iraqis. Moreover, there were several human rights groups and journalists that published their own findings in 2004.

Together they offered a host of valuable clues as to why this institutional "barrel" had gone bad. First, investigators discovered that lawyers inside the Defense and Justice departments as well as the White House, acting on instructions from their civilian superiors, produced interpretations of the Geneva Conventions and U.S. law that deliberately shrank the definitions of "torture" down so far that American military and CIA personnel could use techniques that otherwise would have been deemed violations of U.S. and international law.

Second, investigators found that General Geoffrey Miller was sent by Secretary Rumsfeld to Iraq in September 2003, where General Miller recommended that American commanders overseeing military prison operations in Iraq start employing the aggressive interrogation practices that were being used on Afghan and Arab male prisoners at Guantánamo. Somewhat surprisingly, General Miller later was named by the Pentagon to head the Abu Ghraib prison in the wake of the scandal.

Third, investigators discovered that the intense, persistent pressure imposed on military intelligence personnel by Defense Department officials to generate information about who was launching insurgent assaults on the U.S. occupying forces encouraged those military intelligence officers in turn to put pressure on the military police guarding prisoners to "soften up" the men in their cell blocks. This undercut the military police's own chain of command. At the top of that command chain was a female army general, Janice Karpinski, who claimed that her authority over her military police personnel was undermined by intrusive military intelligence officers. This policy change, the U.S. government's own investigators concluded, dangerously blurred the valuable line between military policing and militarized interrogating. Finally, investigators found that nonmilitary personnel, including CIA operatives and outside contractors hired by the CIA and the Pentagon, were involved in the Abu Ghraib military interrogations in ways that may have fostered a string of reinforcing assumptions that the legal limitations on employing excessive force could be treated cavalierly, seeming to have sent the message: "We're under threat, repelling this threat is urgent, the Geneva Conventions or other legal niceties are slowing down our efforts to act with urgency."

By the end of the U.S.-led war in Iraq, there were 250,000 contractors working for the U.S. government in Iraq. There were more contractor personnel than there were U.S. military personnel. One of the prime contracting companies was CACI-International. CACI's employees were among those assigned to Abu Ghraib to take part in CIA-led interrogations. The company was paid $19 million for its work at Abu Ghraib . Only later was CACI sued by several formerly imprisoned Iraqi men for its employees' participation in their torture (all of those Iraqi men were later released from Abu Ghraib without charge) (Editorial Board, 2015).

Using our feminist curiosity leads us to ask several questions that the U.S. government's investigators failed to ask:

- Did it matter who the women were inside the prison and up and down the larger American military and intelligence hierarchies—low-level police reservists, a captain in the military intelligence unit, a general advising the chief U.S. commander in Iraq?
- Did the nature of the daily personal relationships between the military policemen, including Charles Graner, and their female colleagues—who were a minority at Abu Ghraib—matter?

- Was it significant that so many of the abuses perpetrated on the Iraqi male prisoners were deliberately sexualized, designed to feminize and thus humiliate the prisoners? Was hooding a male prisoner the same (in motivation and in result) as forcing him to simulate oral sex?
- Was it at all relevant that Charles Graner, the oldest and apparently most influential of the low-ranking guards charged, had been accused of physical intimidation by his former wife?
- Was subtle pressure to appear "manly" in a time of war placed on the lawyers in the Defense and Justice departments and in the White House who were ordered to draft guidelines to permit U.S. officials to sidestep the Geneva Conventions outlawing torture? This question too seems to have been left on the investigative teams' shelves to gather dust.

Since the mid-1970s, feminists have been introducing new questions to pose and crafting skills to explain when and why organizations become arenas for sexist abuse. One of the great contributions of the work done by what is often referred to as the "Second Wave" of the international women's movement (that is, feminist activism of the 1960s to 1990s) was to shed light on what breeds sex discrimination and sexual harassment inside organizations as dissimilar as a factory, a stockbrokerage, a legislature, a university, a student movement, and a military (Bowers 2004; Kwon 2000; Murphy 2005; Ogasawara 1998; Stockford 2004; Whitworth 2004). All of the authors of the reports on Abu Ghraib talked about a "climate," an "environment," or a "culture," having been created inside Abu Ghraib that fostered abusive acts. The conditions inside Abu Ghraib were portrayed as having been part of a climate of "confusion," of "chaos." It is important to note that it was feminists who gave us this innovative concept of organizational climate.

When trying to figure out why some women employees in some organizations are promoted, while other women were subjected to sexist jokes, unwanted advances, and retribution for not going along with the jokes or not accepting those advances, feminist lawyers, advocates, and scholars began to look beyond the formal policies and the written rules. They explored something more amorphous but just as potent, and maybe even more so: the set of unofficial presumptions that shapes workplace interactions between men and men and between men and women. They followed the breadcrumbs to the casual, informal interactions between people up and down the organization's ladder. They investigated who drinks with whom after work, who sends sexist jokes to whom over office email, who pins up which sorts of pictures of women in their lockers or next to the coffee machine.

These same feminist investigators used gender analysis to explore what those people in authority did not do. They discovered that inaction is a form of action: "turning a blind eye" is itself a form of action. Practicing neglect, trivialization, and cultivating dismissive attitudes each is an action. Inaction sends out signals to everyone in the organization about what is condoned. Feminists labeled these webs of presumptions, informal interactions, and deliberate inaction as an organization's "climate." As feminists argued successfully in court, it is not sufficient for a stockbrokerage or a college to include anti-sexual-harassment guidelines in its official handbook; employers have to take explicit steps to create a workplace climate in which women are treated with fairness and respect.

By 2004, this feminist explanatory concept—organizational "climate"—had become so accepted by so many analysts that their debt to feminists had been forgotten. Generals Taguba, Jones, and Fay, as well as former defense secretary Schlesinger, may never have taken a women's studies course, but when they were assigned the job of investigating Abu Ghraib they drew on the ideas and investigatory skills crafted for them by feminists.

However, more worrisome than the failure by such investigators to acknowledge their intellectual and political debts was their ignoring the feminist lessons that went hand in hand with the concept of "climate." *The first lesson:* to make sense of any organization, one must dig deep into the group's dominant presumptions about femininity and masculinity. *The second lesson:* one needs to take seriously the experiences of diverse women differently situated in any organization as they try to adapt to, or sometimes resist, those dominant gendered presumptions. One watches and listens to women not because all women are angels, but because paying close attention to diverse women's ideas and actions will shed light on why those men with power act the way they do.

It is not as if the potency of ideas about masculinity and femininity had been totally absent from the U.S. military's thinking prior to the Iraq War. Between 1991 and 2004, there was a string of military scandals that had compelled even those American senior officials who preferred to look the other way to face sexism directly. The first such scandal stemmed from the September 1991 gathering of American navy pilots and Defense Department senior officials at a Hilton hotel in Las Vegas. Male aircraft pilots (all officers) are called "Tailhookers." In the fall of 1991, they were fresh from their victory in the first Gulf War. One of their rituals was to line a hotel corridor and physically assault every woman who stepped off the elevator. They made the "mistake" in September, 1991 of assaulting a woman navy helicopter pilot who was serving as an aide to an admiral. When she complained to her superior, the admiral, he dismissed her complaint. Yet she persevered. Within months, members of Congress and the media were telling the public about "Tailhook"—why it happened and who tried to cover it up (Office of the Inspector General, 2003). Close on the heels of the navy's "Tailhook" scandal came the army's Aberdeen training base sexual harassment scandal, followed by other revelations of gay bashing, sexual harassment, and rapes by American male military personnel (Enloe 1993, 2000).

Then in September 1995, the rape of a local school girl by two American male marines and a sailor in Okinawa sparked public demonstrations, the formation of new Okinawan women's advocacy groups, and more U.S. congressional investigation (Enloe 2000). At the start of the twenty-first century, American media began to notice the patterns of international trafficking in Eastern European and Filipino women around American bases in South Korea, prompting official embarrassment in Washington (embarrassment that had not been demonstrated earlier when American base commanders were classically dismissive of a prostitution industry organized locally to service those commanders' own male soldiers, because it employed "merely" local South Korean women). And in 2003, three new American military gendered (and frequently sexualized) scandals caught Washington policymakers' attention: four American male soldiers returning from combat missions in Afghanistan murdered their female partners at Fort Bragg, North Carolina; a pattern of sexual harassment and rape by male cadets of female cadets—and superiors' refusal to treat these acts seriously—was revealed at the U.S. Air Force Academy; and at least sixty American women soldiers returning from tours of duty in Kuwait and Iraq testified that they had been sexually assaulted by their male colleagues there—once again, with senior officers choosing inaction and advising the American women soldiers to "get over it" (Jargon 2003; Lutz and Elliston 2004; Moffeit and Herder 2004).

Carol Burke, a professor of folklore, taught at the U.S. Naval Academy at Annapolis. When the evidence of abuses perpetrated in Abu Ghraib started to become news, she immediately drew the parallels between what had gone on inside the prison and what she herself had witnessed routinely among American male midshipmen at the naval academy: men using feminized rituals of hazing to try to humiliate other male cadets. She found that these humiliation rituals among male midshipmen simultaneously reinforced the collective contempt with which anything "tainted" with femininity was held. Even the midshipmen's use of women's underwear and coerced sexual acts of men on men were identical to what went on inside the U.S.-run Abu Ghraib (Burke 2004, 2006).

So it should have come as no surprise to senior uniformed and civilian policymakers seeking to make sense of the abuses perpetrated in Abu Ghraib that a culture of sexism had come to permeate many sectors of U.S. military life. If they had thought about what they had all learned in the last thirteen years—from Tailhook, Aberdeen, Fort Bragg, Okinawa, South Korea, and the U.S. Air Force Academy—they should have put the workings of masculinity and femininity at the top of their investigatory agendas. They should have made feminist curiosity one of their own principal tools. Perhaps Tillie Fowler, a Republican Congressional representative from Florida, did suggest to her colleagues that they think about these military scandals when they began to delve into Abu Ghraib. Tillie Fowler had been a principal investigator on the team that looked into the rapes (and their cover-ups) at the U.S. Air Force Academy. Because of her leadership in that role, Fowler was appointed to the commission headed by James Schlesinger investigating Abu Ghraib. If she raised the commonalities between the Air Force Academy's culture of sexism and that of the Abu Ghraib prison, did her male colleagues take her suggestion seriously?

Perhaps ultimately the American investigators did not make use of the feminist lessons and tools because they imagined that the lessons of Tailhook, Aberdeen, Fort Bragg, Okinawa, South Korea, and the Air Force Academy were relevant only when all the perpetrators of sexual abuse are men and all the victims are women. Perhaps they ignored their knowledge of the sexualized hazing practices common in American military organizations (and in fraternities and sports teams at American colleges) because, after all, those could be dismissed as "boys being boys" and could be imagined as having no serious consequences on either the men being hazed or the women implicitly being denigrated.

They might have assumed that the presence of Lynndie England and the other women in Abu Ghraib's military police unit made the feminist tools sharpened in those earlier gendered military scandals inappropriate for their current investigation. But the lesson of Tailhook and the other military scandals was not that the politics of masculinity and femininity matter only when men are the perpetrators and women are the victims. Instead, the deeper lesson of all those other military scandals is that one must always ask, "Has this organization (or this system of interlocking organizations) become masculinized in ways that privilege certain forms of masculinity, feminize its opposition, and trivialize most forms of femininity?"

With this core gender question in mind, we might uncover significant dynamics operating in Abu Ghraib and in the American military and civilian organizations that were supposed to be supervising the prison's personnel. American military police and their military and CIA intelligence colleagues might have been guided by their own masculinized fears of humiliation when they forced Iraqi men to go naked for days, to wear women's underwear, and to masturbate in front of each other and American women guards.

That is, the Americans' belief in an allegedly "exotic," frail Iraqi masculinity, fraught with fears of nakedness and homosexuality, might not have been the chief motivator for the American police and intelligence personnel; it may have been their own homegrown American sense of masculinity's fragility—how easily manliness can be feminized and thus discredited—that prompted them to craft these prison humiliations. Either belief could encourage the guards to wield feminization as a technique of prisoner humiliation. In this distorted masculinized scenario, the presence of women serving as military police might have proved especially useful. Choreographing the women guards' feminized roles so that they could act as ridiculing feminized spectators of male prisoners might have been imagined to intensify the demasculinizing demoralization. As histories of international conflicts in Vietnam, Rwanda, and Western Europe have revealed, dominant men trying to use women in ways that undermine the masculinized self-esteem of rival men is not new.

What about the American women soldiers themselves? In the U.S. military of 2004, women constituted 15 percent of active duty personnel, 17 percent of all reserves and the National Guard, and a surprising 24 percent of the army reserves alone. From the very time these particular young women joined this military police unit, they, like their fellow male recruits, probably sought to fit into the group. If the unit's evolving culture—perhaps fostered by their superiors for the sake of "morale" and "unit cohesion"—became a micro-culture that privileged a certain form of masculinized humor, racism, and bravado, each woman would have had to decide how to deal with that in order to "get along." At least some of the women reservists might have decided to join in, to play the roles assigned to them in order to gain the hoped-for reward of their male colleagues' acceptance. The fact that the Abu Ghraib prison was grossly understaffed during the fall of 2003 (too few guards for the spiraling numbers of Iraqi detainees), that it was isolated from other military operations, and that its residents endured daily and nightly mortar attacks would only serve to intensify the pressures on each soldier to gain acceptance from those unit members who seemed to represent the group's dominant masculinized culture.

And what about the fact that Lynndie England entered into a sexual liaison with Charles Graner? We need to treat this as more than merely a "lack of discipline." Looking back on the masculinized and sexualized climate inside the both internally troubled and externally besieged prison, Janis Karpinski, the army reserve general in charge of the prison, recalled how, over the years of her career, she had seen so many young women soldiers "seek protection" from older, more senior male soldiers, usually with those men more than willing to serve as their female subordinates' "protectors" (Karpinski 2005). It would be more useful to ask about the cause-and-effect dynamics between these soldiers' sexual behaviors and their abuses of Iraqi prisoners (including the staged photographs). Feminists have taught us never to brush off sexual relations as if they have nothing to do with organizational and political practices.

Then there is the masculinization of the military interrogators' organizational culture, the masculinization of the CIA's field operatives and their private contractors, as well as the ideas about "manliness" shaping the entire U.S. political system in the early 2000s. Many men and women—lawyers, generals, cabinet members, elected officials—

knew full well that aggressive interrogation techniques violated both the spirit and the language of the Geneva Conventions, the UN Convention against Torture (which the U.S. Congress had ratified in 1994), and U.S. federal laws against torture. Yet during the months of waging wars in Afghanistan and Iraq, most of these men and women kept silent. Feminists have taught us always to be curious about silence. This should prompt us to ask: Did any of the American men involved in interrogations keep silent because they were afraid of being labeled "soft" or "weak," thereby jeopardizing their status as "manly" men? We need also to discover if any of the women who knew better kept silent because they were afraid that they would be labeled "feminine," thus risking being deemed by their Congressional, bureaucratic, or military colleagues to be untrustworthy, mere outsiders.

We are not going to get to the bottom of the tortures perpetrated by Americans at Abu Ghraib unless we make use of a feminist curiosity and unless we revisit the feminist lessons derived from the scandals that have been revealed at the Tailhook convention, Fort Bragg, the U.S. Naval Academy, Okinawa, and the Air Force Academy. A feminist curiosity, combined with those lessons, might shed a harsh light on an entire American military institutional culture and maybe even the climate of contemporary American political life. That military culture and that political climate together have profound implications for both Americans and for all those citizens in countries where the U.S. military is being held up as a model to emulate as they modernize their own armed forces.

Those citizens being encouraged to adopt the American military's culture and political climate—in Central and Eastern Europe's newest members of NATO, as well as in South Korea, Japan, the Philippines, Afghanistan, and Iraq—might find it valuable to consider these feminist-informed lessons.

Let's return to that June 2006 newspaper. There was a third article in the newspaper that morning that a reader, sipping a morning cup of coffee in the safety of her or his own kitchen, might have noticed. The *New York Times* editors made this article much more prominent than the others. This article dealt with the rapidly unfolding story of assaults by U.S. male marines in the Iraqi town of Haditha on November 19, 2005.

The alleged assaults took place a year after Abu Ghraib dominated the world's headlines and two years after the infamous photos were taken by gloating American guards. Eight months later investigations into what happened that November in Haditha began to become known to the public. Now, in mid-2006, a story was unfolding that suggested that a group of marines retaliated violently after one of their fellow marines had been killed by a roadside bomb. They allegedly killed perhaps as many as two dozen Iraqi civilians, including an old man in a wheelchair, women inside their own homes, and children as young as four years old. Later, seemingly with the support of some of their superior officers, these marines claimed that the Iraqis had been killed by an insurgent's bomb or in intense combat. Forensic evidence that was later revealed, however, suggested that these twenty-four Iraqi civilians had been shot at close range by the marines (Broder et al. 2006).

Haditha is a town in the sparsely populated Iraqi province of Anbar. Over the past two decades Anbar's local culture had become both more militarized and more masculinized; those two intertwined processes, already underway, seemed to speed up even more following the U.S. invasion in 2003, as the predominantly Sunni population mobilized to fight its own insurgency against the U.S. military occupation. In November 2005, these Iraqi processes met another process of masculinized militarization head on—this process was American. According to some American observers, the U.S. Marines, who had just rotated into Anbar, replacing the previous army troops there, were determined to impose a tougher, more masculinized operational discipline on the rebellious province.

The U.S. Marines' culture of masculinity would replace—and presumably be more effective against the insurgents than—the U.S. Army's allegedly weaker culture of masculinity (Burns 2006). A subsequent investigation by a senior army commander found that marine officers, including those not physically on the scene that deadly November day, had laid the cultural groundwork for the massacre: they had created a particular "climate." One Pentagon official explained the cultural message that the marine officers had sent down through the ranks about how American soldiers should view Iraqis in Anbar: "In their eyes, they didn't believe anyone was innocent. . . . Either you were an active participant, or you were complicit" (Cloud 2006).

"Haditha" became a shorthand for yet another toxic stew of gendered globalized militarized dynamics. Though several U.S. marines were charged, none went to jail for the killings of Iraqi civilians at Haditha (Enloe 2010). By 2015, the residents of Haditha, mostly Sunni Muslims, were caught again in the middle of militarized violence, this time between the male fighters of ISIS and the male fighters of Iraq's government-sponsored Shiite militias.

Some members of the U.S. Congress compared the November 2005 massacre at Haditha and its apparent cover-up to the U.S. military massacre of civilians over thirty years ago, in 1968, in the Vietnamese village of My Lai. Other American legislators, trying to assess preliminary evidence of the seemingly out-of-control and violent behavior of lower-ranking soldiers and the attempted cover-ups by superiors, drew analogies to a more recent scandal, Abu Ghraib (Oppel 2006).

All of these news stories—some making the front page, others buried by editors on the inside pages—were breaking at the same time, furthermore, as international legal experts were calling on the U.S. government to close down its military prison and interrogation center in Guantánamo. European legal scholars and investigators had concluded that U.S. military practices at Guantánamo stood in violation of the agreed-upon international norms governing warfare and rules protecting human rights (Sciolino 2006).

Thus, evidence gathered between 2004 and 2006 suggested that the U.S. militarized practices at Guantánamo, at Bagram, and at Abu Ghraib were linked, gendered, and globalized.

In April 2004, a year after the U.S. government had launched its massive military invasion of Iraq, a series of shocking photographs of American soldiers abusing Iraqi prisoners began appearing on television news programs, the front pages of newspapers, and Internet sites around the world. The revelations of Abu Ghraib quickly took on the attributes of a globalized event.

Abu Ghraib was globalized, first, in that it exposed actions by military personnel and their civilian superiors that were in blatant violation of internationally agreed-upon norms of state behavior—norms written into international law and ratified by the U.S. government. Many people around the globe for the first time read paragraphs of the UN Convention against Torture, and Other Cruel, Inhuman or Degrading Treatment or Punishment, even though it had been adopted in 1984 and signed by their governments in their name. While often referred to simply as the "Convention against Torture," its full title makes clear its far broader prohibition. The U.S. government, on behalf of all U.S. citizens, signed the Convention. The impetus for its creation in the early

1980s was the international revulsion at the news of the use of torture by military regimes in Chile and Argentina—something that was not uncommon in dozens of other countries ruled by authoritarian and militarized governments, which claimed that enemies within and without could be dealt with only by extraordinary and, if necessary, violent state methods. An international consensus rejected this justification. The Convention against Torture was the product of that historic consensus (Sands 2005).

Second, Abu Ghraib became globalized in that it sparked a worldwide discussion—one that is still going on today—about the ethics of waging war, about the definitions of torture, about the accountability of intelligence services, about urgency, about fear. During the spring and summer of 2004, as the evidence of what had occurred in the cell blocks of Abu Ghraib almost a year earlier mounted, ordinary citizens found themselves talking with friends about "sexual humiliation," "sleep deprivation," "stress positions," and "psychological torture." Many listened to, or read for the first time, detailed discussions by legal and political experts about what counts as "torture," whether torture "works," how ordinary individuals could be desensitized (and by whom) to the point that they could become torturers, and how torture undermines democratic cultures and the rule of law. In the age of satellite television and around-the-clock Internet communication, this became a globalized conversation.

Third, what American personnel—military personnel and militarized civilians—had done inside Abu Ghraib was globalized in the sense that people from scores of countries began to see themselves as having a stake in understanding and critiquing the causes and actions that were gradually revealed. Not everyone agreed that such critical national self-reflection was necessary. In fact, there were people who argued that since the September 11, 2001, attacks, preventing terrorism justified all means of capture, detention, and interrogation. The stakes were too high, they contended, to allow the norms of legal conventions and formal treaties to get in the way of effective prevention. On the other side, often in the same country, there were people who felt that the stakes were too high to treat Abu Ghraib as merely a one-country story. They saw the fundamental character of the twenty-first century's international political system as being at stake: Would everyone revert to imagining that abusive militarism in one country did not jeopardize the cultures of law and human rights and decency in all others, especially when the government claiming the exception was itself so culturally and militarily influential?

This stream of globalized thinking was especially meaningful in those countries, such as Chile, Argentina, South Africa, Guatemala, Greece, Turkey, and South Korea, where torture committed by militarized regimes was still fresh in the minds of many citizens and where the work to undo the cultural and structural damage inflicted by those authoritarian regimes was still going on even twenty years after the generals had been forced to relinquish their power.

Fourth, in the months and years following the disclosure of the prisoner abuse, the Abu Ghraib scandal became globalized because the very setting in which the abuses occurred was internationalized: one state, the United States, had preemptively invaded the territory of another state, Iraq, with the officially expressed intent of imposing international norms of democratic political and legal behavior on that state. That justification was offered in the name of globalizing those norms. In the process, however, the American officials of the George W. Bush administration tried to militarize globalization. That is, they claimed that the goal of globalizing democratic and rule-of-law norms could be achieved only through military actions. This is a justification that can seem appealing to many government officials in many countries—and to the civilian voters who support them.

Fifth, and last, the abusive treatment of Iraqi prisoners in Abu Ghraib turned out to be globalized in the sense that American defense and intelligence officials had purposefully transported ideas around the world—ideas about who was not worthy of prisoners' rights, ideas about whose interrogation was "urgent," and ideas about what techniques of interrogation were allowable and "effective."

Thus, Lynndie England was never "the story." She is interesting. She deserves to be fully understood. But so too do Janis Karpinski, the former and current wives of Charles Graner, General Barbara Fast, Captain Carolyn Wood, and the women who served as military and contract interrogators and interpreters in both Guantánamo and Abu Ghraib. Paying attention to diverse militarized women's actions, motivations, assumptions, and immediate as well as distant relationships to male senior commanders and male civilian policymakers can help us see how militarized feminization operates, who wields it, who is complicit in it and why, whom it serves, and what larger cultural goals it promotes.

It is by tracking the gendered assumptions about how to wield feminization to humiliate male prisoners inside Abu Ghraib, not in isolation, but with the understanding that those assumptions were linked to the ideas, assumptions, and policies shaping detention and interrogation practices at Bagram and Guantánamo—and the unknown number of secret prisons used by the U.S. government around the world—that we are likely to get a clearer picture of why "Abu Ghraib" happened—and whether it will happen again.

CHAPTER 7

DEMILITARIZING
YOUR CLOSET

Do You Wear "Camo"?

The Women of Color Resource Center (WCRC) is not what most experts think of as a site of research on militarization and demilitarization. But that oversight may be due to many militarization experts' narrow notions of "expertise." The WCRC is an energetic organization located in downtown Oakland, California, that challenges racism in all its myriad sexist forms and develops programs for Asian American, African American, Native American, and Latina women in the San Francisco Bay Area.

When the Center's members began to question the links between racism, militarism, and sexism, they tried to think of an event that would be engaging rather than off-putting. As the director of the WCRC's small antimilitarism project, Christine Ahn wanted to find a topic that would nudge young women toward thinking about their own possible complicity in the processes of militarization. In 2004, she began mulling over the meanings of "camo." Camo is the popular nickname for the fashion of turning the military's camouflaged designs into tank tops, shorts, pants, knapsacks, even condoms. Ahn wondered whether the many young people she knew who were buying and wearing this "hip" fashion—her peers—had thought about the implications of their style choices. Christine Ahn went into action. She organized what might have been the first-ever antimilitarism fashion show.

The WCRC took over the refurbished theater in downtown Oakland in 2005, and by an evening in late May, the lobby and the theater were alive with displays, music, performers, and the conversations of a lively audience. Christine Ahn had invited a wide array of Bay Area groups—ranging from young male hip-hop fashion designers to Code Pink, a network of feminist peace activists. They were all crowded into the lobby, displaying their wares and talking with other attendees. Inside the theater, the show was about to begin. The lights went down, and the disc jockey started to spin her records. The master of ceremonies was a tall African American woman, herself a performance poet. She was soon joined by local rappers talking about war and peace. The stage began to fill with camo. There was camo casual wear, there were camo ball gowns.

Then there were "blasts from the past." One participant told the story of khaki—how khaki wasn't coined by The Gap but was an Afghan word to describe the distinctive color of that country's stark hillsides, which the British imperial army adopted for their own uniform colors but only after their red-coated troops were defeated in their initial efforts to subdue the region's less dramatically attired tribal fighters. Khaki as a popular color has its roots in military conquest. The lights then focused on a well-known and longtime Bay Area Latina activist who strode to the front of the stage wearing a classic 1940s outfit—hat, gloves, brass-buttoned coat, and pumps—all in patriotic red, white, and blue. She was followed by a slender young woman wearing nothing but a bikini. The boisterous audience cheered. Then the poet MC told them that the bikini was created by a designer who wanted to exploit the international popular interest in the U.S. atomic bomb testing in the Pacific, which rendered Bikini, an island, uninhabitable. The audience uttered a collective gasp.

That was the goal of Christine Ahn and her WCRC colleagues. She didn't want to lecture these California women and men about what to think about the camo in their closets. She hoped instead that the fashion show would start them thinking and developing their own thoughts about militarization and about their own personal relationships to militarization (www.wcrc.org; www.genuinesecurity.org).

Thousands of miles away, in Turkey, other local activists were organizing their own innovative event—one they hoped would raise ordinary civilians' consciousness about the dailiness of militarization and generate new awareness of that often invisible process. They didn't choose a fashion show. These Turkish activists, women and men, many of them feminists and anti-conscription activists, instead organized a militarism tour. They called their event "Militourism."

Taking people on bus and walking tours around Istanbul and Ankara, they pointed out buildings where every day some small or major strand of militarized Turkish life was woven. Most of these places were the sort that civilians passed every day without noticing and without thinking about what was going on inside, about what was being done there in their names, for their protection, for the "good of the nation." It is not as if Turkish women and men are unconscious of the central role that the military has played since the 1920s in shaping both public policy and national myths of unity, modernity, masculine duty, and the secular state. The Turkish military has made itself too prominent to be overlooked. Yet the organizers of the annual Militourism events wanted to make even clearer to their fellow citizens that both the military and practices of militarized living were more diverse and more "ordinary" than perhaps even the reader of the daily newspapers realized (Altinay 2004; Mater 2005).

In Israel, a small group of middle-aged Jewish women (and now several young women and men in their new youth group) have come together, one by one, and call themselves New Profile. Out of their concern that children's lives were being simultaneously infused with racism and militarized, they tried to build bridges with Israeli academics involved in the country's educational system. It has turned out to be hard work. They also decided to take their messages about militarism into modest local sites. These women created a traveling exhibit to reveal how ideas about soldiering, about the country's recent past, about the military's centrality in Israeli life are even inserted into primary school children's education. The exhibit wasn't flashy. It was assembled by the New Profile women themselves by looking at what their own children, grandchildren, nieces, and nephews were being shown in schools and in contemporary children's books. They mounted their findings on five-foot-high folding boards. The women have to be able to carry these boards around the country, to Haifa and Tel Aviv, as well as to Jerusalem, and assemble the exhibit without fuss. A New Profile member sat by the exhibit wherever they got permission to set it up—in schools, in local community centers, at conferences. She did not lecture the people who came to look at its images and captions; she was there to answer any visitors' questions or just to engage in conversation.

At first glance, some people who came thought that the exhibit was in praise of the military. Only on closer inspection did they see the problematic relationships and ideas being revealed. There was a guest book, too, in which anyone who came to look at the exhibit could share her or his own reactions. Underlying New Profile's modest exhibit was an ambitious goal: to inspire their fellow citizens, especially their fellow Jewish citizens (today, 25 percent of Israel's citizens are non-Jews, mostly Palestinian Israelis, but also Bedouin, Druze, and diverse foreign workers), to weigh the costs of having created or consented to such a racism-infused and deeply militarized public culture, to think too about how guns and soldiering had become so normalized in their daily lives (www.newprofile.org; www.cordaid.org/en/projects/campaign-for-gun -free-kitchen-tables/109676).

Being analytically clear, visually creative, and collectively determined have been common hallmarks of feminist peace activists trying to show that militarism is not the only package of ideas that can shape people's relationships to each other.

In May 2015, a group of twenty-nine women from fifteen countries did what no one thought was possible: they walked from North Korea, across the heavily militarized so-called Demilitarized Zone ("DMZ") into South Korea. Among the walkers were three Nobel Peace Prize recipients—Liberia's Leymah Gbowee, Northern Ireland's Mairead Maguire, and the American Jody Williams—as well as Okinawan anti-militarism activist Suzuyo Takazato; filmmaker Abigail Disney; veterans-for-peace activist Ann Wright; peace studies scholar Kozue Akibayashi; and feminist activists Christine Ahn, Gwyn Kirk, and Gloria Steinem. They named their peace project Women Cross DMZ.

Being experienced feminist-informed activists, the participants were ready for the ridicule that was certain to come: that they were naïve, that they were dupes of the North Korean regime, and that they had no power to change anything. The same sorts of dismissive criticisms had been aimed at women peace activists for the last hundred years, since other women traveled to the Hague in 1915 to protest the militarized violence of World War I. In response, the participants in the north-to-south walk explained that their walk generated global media attention to the lack of a peace treaty to formally end the 1950s Korean War and that it provided hope to Korean families divided by the mutual militarizations and the DMZ for two generations. Moreover, the feminist peace walkers explained, even the complex process of obtaining multiple permissions for the walk from the U.S. military command and officials in Pyongyang and Seoul had created a relationship of cooperation that was groundbreaking. That is, they were not naïve. They were practical in their creative peacemaking (www.womencrossdmz.org).

In Bogota, Colombia, a new government department devoted to reintegrating insurgent fighters into civilian society was launched in 2011. Its civil servants work in small crowded offices, two or three workers sharing each cubicle, with posters on the walls and glass partitions meant to show the happiness that awaits a man or woman who leaves behind their militarized life. They have had coffee mugs made imprinted with their motto: "Paso a Paso." Step by step. They have learned that demilitarizing one's life does not come in leaps. It comes step by excruciating step, hardest for those men and women who have been living as fighters for years. Taking each step can be difficult; it calls for learning new ways to relate to other men and other women, and for crafting new understandings of themselves.

From trial and error, Colombia's current reintegration workers have developed their own lessons. One of the most important, they have explained, is to reconnect male fighters with the civilian women who used to be in their lives, especially the women with whom they have had children. For many men, the step-by-step demilitarizing journey can be eased by their learning to be a caring father. A man laying down his gun to take up the hand of a small child is one of the reintegrators' most powerful images. To actually turn this image into a reality, of course, has required reintegration workers to persuade those children's mothers, women who have been struggling during the armed conflict to raise children on their own, to let these male ex-fighters back into their lives. Not all women have been eager for such a reconnection.

These small-scale reintegrating efforts were happening at the same time as a crucial Colombian peace agreement was being hammered out in Havana between male delegates of the main guerrilla force, the FARC, and male delegates of the government. Despite the masculinized character of the Havana peace negotiations, Colombian women activists organizing across the country's racialized boundaries and from scores of local groups had managed to get their voices heard and at least some of their issues on the table. Many Colombian feminists, for instance, had been working for years to ensure that those male fighters who have perpetrated sexual abuses against women during the conflict would not be granted immunity. Many feminist activists, consequently, have remained skeptical of any moves toward carte blanche reintegration of former fighters (www.reintegration.gov.co/en/agency; www.humanas.cl; www.wilpf.org/colombia).

A fashion show, a city tour, a small display of children's books, building solidarity in defiance of racism, a walk across a mine field, a micro-level reintegration effort, and a campaign to have women's issues put on a masculinized negotiating table. These are not the usual activities studied by those analyzing militarization or laying out the steps for effective demilitarization. Instead, what most conventional experts on demilitarization direct their attention to are shrinking government defense budgets, large-scale disarmament, formal peace agreements between major parties to armed conflicts, and generals stepping back from—or being pushed out of—state power.

Each of these seven "conventional" processes matter—and each of them is gendered. Nonetheless, the feminist-informed peace activists in San Francisco, Oakland, Istanbul, Ankara, Tel Aviv, Haifa, the Korean DMZ, and Bogota who created these less-visible demilitarizing efforts did so because they had become convinced that, if militarization had taken myriad and often-unnoticed actions to move forward in their societies, then demilitarization, the reversal of that process, would start only when the invisible became visible, when the naturalized was made problematic, and when the impossible is shown to be possible.

Members of each group have believed in the power of ideas—ideas about what is stylish, what is educational, what is serious, what is naïve, what is seductive, and what is normal. They have believed that popularly held ideas—not just interests, policies, or institutions—have been a prime source of militarization. Thus, all of these women working in such different ways for demilitarization had become convinced that only through raising new questions in the minds of their fellow citizens could fresh conversations begin—conversations that might eventually turn into pressures for sustainable demilitarization.

Demilitarization: Today we are learning—often painfully, and usually reluctantly—that demilitarization may be one of the toughest transformative processes to carry through to completion. To demilitarize any society—or simply a town, an organization, a television network, a political party, a family, a company, a school, or a sense of oneself—turns out to require changes many of us would rather avoid. We want to don our camo shorts if they are deemed fashionable. Out of fear, we fall into racism as we lash out at entire categories of people in the wake of violence by only a few. We feel comfortable trusting that our young children are learning healthy lessons in their schools. We like the buzz of excitement when jet fighters roar overhead to open a sports season. We want to keep cashing our paychecks from our employers, even if their executives bid on defense contracts. We prefer to hope for the best in all-male peace negotiations. We want to hold our marriages together without scrutinizing our partner's classified weapons work. We want to continue to be accepted by our fellow citizens as patriots. Demilitarization will call on us to scrutinize our daily desires.

Many demilitarizing actions go unnoticed. They usually are actions taken by individuals without fanfare. But that lack of public attention doesn't necessarily make demilitarizing steps easy to take, particularly if militarism's beliefs, values, and practices have become normal or even glorified:

- A Parisian woman refuses to blame all refugees for an act of violence in her city.
- In the wake of a terrorist attack in Beirut, a Lebanese shopkeeper continues to take pride in his city as a multicultural haven.
- A South Korean prodemocracy activist decides to critique how she and her fellow activists adopted militaristic ideas and strategies even as they sought to topple the country's military regime (Kwon 2000).
- A Chilean middle-aged woman buys new sneakers for her elderly mother and aunt so they can run away from police tear gas when they take part in an antimilitary rally.

- A nineteen-year-old Jewish Israeli woman decides to resist her army's conscription notice, even while most of her friends are accepting theirs, because, she explains, after volunteering for local groups seeking to support abused women, she now realizes that by becoming a soldier she would violate her anti-violence principles as a feminist (Halili 2006).
- A Puerto Rican woman gains new self-confidence when joining with her neighbors to force the U.S. Navy to withdraw from its military base and stop using her island of Vieques as a bombing range (Ferguson and Mironesco 2008; Lutz 2009).
- An Argentine mother decides that, even though the military has been ousted from power, she will not give up pressuring the now-civilian elected government to bring the generals to justice (Arditti 1999).
- A Burmese voter casts a ballot for a poet rather than a general in a crucial election.
- A Canadian woman living in Winnipeg, Manitoba, decides to speak out against Ottawa's plan to conduct urban warfare military maneuvers in her city.
- An Egyptian feminist refuses to give the military generals credit for enhancing her sense of security.
- The father of an American Latino soldier who was killed in Iraq decides that he cannot grieve in private, so he visits high schools with large Latino enrollments to speak to students about the reasons Latino young people should not enlist in the U.S. military.

Some of these individual actions remain just that. The person may be scorned or admired now and then by his or her family and colleagues, but otherwise few people pay any attention to that person's decision and the reasoning behind it. Occasionally, however, enough individuals discover that they are not alone in their critical thinking and actions, that they can create a group; perhaps, over time, enough small groups connect with each other that together they become a more sprawling network, a "movement."

On even fewer occasions, news of such individual and collective decisions and actions can travel across national boundaries and become globalized. This happened with the Mothers and Grandmothers of the

Plaza de Mayo, a group of older women who stood up to the military in Argentina, insisting after the end of military rule that senior officers be held accountable for their abuses. News of their actions traveled to Turkey, where it inspired Turkish women to organize as mothers calling on the militarized government to provide news of their missing sons and daughters (Baydar and Ivegen 2006). This is similar to what has happened over the last century as individuals (mostly men) in many countries have resisted compulsory military service ("conscription" or "the draft"), have compared experiences, and often joined by women supporters who become integral to the movement, have created international networks of support for conscientious objectors (Cinar and Usterci 2009).

Globalized demilitarization: A good example is the social movement that led to the 1997 international Mine Ban Treaty. While this agreement was arrived at between governments, those governments came together to hammer out the agreement and then to sign its pledge to stop producing and using land mines because of the educational and political lobbying done by nongovernmental activists. Jody Williams, a young Vermont woman, and the organization she founded, the International Campaign to Ban Landmines (ICBL), were awarded the prestigious Nobel Peace Prize in 1997 for their work around the world to convince government officials that land mines should be banned. They had witnessed and documented the devastating consequences of land mines for women, men, and children—most of them noncombatants (www.icbl .org; Stiehm 2006). A rural Cambodian or Mozambique child with an artificial leg became the global symbol of what land mines do—they can lie unmarked in deadly wait beneath the soil of a farmer's field or along a rural path, lie in wait for years after the warring sides have signed peace agreements.

The Mine Ban Treaty was signed in Ottawa in 1997. The Canadian foreign minister had taken the lead among government officials in the final stage of the international campaign to turn the grassroots effort into a multilateral agreement among governments (Beier 2004). Although one of its own citizens was awarded the Nobel Peace Prize in recognition of her campaigning for the treaty, the U.S. government has continued to refuse to sign or ratify it. Resistance from the Pentagon proved decisive. Defense officials argued—and members of the White

House and the Senate (in the U.S. system international treaties must be ratified by the Senate) agreed—that land mines were too valuable, for instance in separating North from South Korea, to be given up.

Today 133 governments have signed and ratified the Mine Ban Treaty. Globalized activist work still goes on to pressure the non-signing governments to sign the treaty and to monitor the ratifying governments. There are feminists involved in this continuing campaign since they found that land mines are gendered: first, rural women and men in mined regions are affected in their daily lives differently because they play different roles in farming, traveling to markets, and making community decisions about who has the knowledge to plan any de-mining efforts; second, inside international anti-mine aid groups it is often presumed that only men have the expertise to organize complex de-mining operations; and, third, within those governments that have refused to ratify the anti-mine treaty, it is often deemed "soft" and "feminine" for an official to object to the continued deployment of land mines.

There are a number of international—that is, government-to-government—agreements designed to limit the barbarity of warfare and to stop the spread of instruments of violence. Some of these agreements might be seen as efforts less to demilitarize the world than to globalize the ethics of militarized behavior. Most prominent among these globalizing efforts are:

- the Geneva Conventions
- the Convention against Torture and Other Cruel, Inhuman or Degrading Treatment or Punishment
- the Mine Ban Treaty
- the Convention on the Rights of the Child
- the Treaty of Rome, establishing the International Criminal Court (the world's first permanent "war crimes tribunal")
- the Arms Trade Treaty

The effectiveness of these international agreements depends on national governments' officials signing and ratifying them. Signing is often politically easier for a government to do than ratifying, since by ratifying a treaty that government can be held internationally responsible for implementing the pledges at the core of the treaty. Even after a sufficient number of the world's governments have signed and ratified one of these agreements, achieving implementation and enforcement depends on the political commitment and will of government officials and attentive citizens (Reichberg, Syse, and Begby 2006; www.peace women.org).

How many high schools include the study of even half of these treaties in their curricula? How many colleges and universities require students to take courses that spell out the history and implementation of these agreements? How many law schools devote time to these legal commitments? Do many legislators consider it part of their political responsibility to challenge their governments to ratify them and then to enforce them? When do voters weigh the appeal of a candidate on the basis of her or his stand on any of these treaties?

If the answer to any of these questions in any country is "not many," "almost never," then it is worth asking a follow-up question: why?

Such inattentiveness may suggest that globalization is not as rampant as we usually presume. Globalization, in other words, seems to lose its momentum when what is being globalized are restraints on war waging and on preparations for war waging.

Demilitarization, in other words, calls for more than silencing the cannons. Those working for demilitarization with feminist analytical tools have discovered that dominant ideas about manliness have to be addressed (Conway 2012; Munn 2007; Parpart and Zalewski 2008). For example, one of the most widespread programs that the United Nations introduces in societies that are trying to implement precarious peace accords is called Disarmament, Demobilization, and Reintegration, or "DDR" as post-conflict field workers routinely call it. Nowadays DDR is seen by its proponents as integral to international peacekeeping in countries trying not only to end wartime violence, but to lay the groundwork for a sustainable peace. DDR is a tough political assignment. When attempts to implement it were tried in Northern Ireland, El Salvador, Guatemala, East Timor, Congo, Liberia, Sierra Leone, Mozambique, and Kosovo, it was vigorously resisted. People who have found safety, influence, and even a deep sense of identity in their possession of guns, sometimes walking and sleeping with those guns for years, are not likely to easily surrender them to international workers simply to garner what seem to be dubious offers of food, medical care, and training for new peacetime jobs. Guns have come to mean too much to those who hold them. That meaning is often infused with ideas about manliness.

Conflict-zone officials and field workers in the early years of DDR saw the gun holders as just "soldiers," "combatants," "militiamen," or "insurgents." They didn't see them explicitly as men or as boys. It has taken interventions—not always welcomed—by feminists in nongovernmental organizations to expose what was missing in this conventional DDR approach: a curiosity about masculinities. These soldiers, combatants, militiamen, and insurgents frequently were men proud of their wartime status as gun-holding masculinized men. Unless those ideas about—and needs for—approved masculinity were effectively addressed, lasting disarmament, demobilization, and reintegration were not likely to be achieved. The result: demilitarization would be partial, superficial, and short lived (Farr 2006; Farr and Gebre-Wold 2002).

If and when fighters, a great majority of whom are young men, need to be weaned away from their guns and reintegrated into civilian life, the lessons learned by the Colombians may prove especially useful. What feminist demilitarization specialists are teaching us is that it will take serious thinking about men's relationships to women and about alternative masculinities to effectively demilitarize these diverse men—male fighters from northern Nigeria's Boko Haram, fighters in the several insurgent forces operating in northern Mali, men wielding guns in Mexico's rival drug gangs, the men active in the American armed right-wing group Posse Comitatas, fighters in Burma's multiple ethnic insurgencies, men who have spent years perpetrating violence in eastern Congo, combatants in eastern Ukraine's break-away army, foreign fighters who have joined ISIS in Syria and Iraq, the men who fill the ranks of Iraq's Shiite militias, as well as Afghan, Pakistani, and men of other nationalities who have been fighting for Al Qaeda.

Lepa Mladjenovic, one of the founders of the Belgrade Women in Black, is a longtime activist working to end violence against women. She explained to an audience in New York in 2005 how a decade after the signing of the 1995 Dayton Accords, the internationally brokered agreement intended to end the war in Bosnia, men's relationships to guns had disturbingly changed in her city. As a volunteer in groups supporting women subjected to violence, she had witnessed over the past ten years of "peace" an increase in men's use of guns and an increase in men's access to guns. This was the opposite of what was supposed to happen after the peace accords. Lepa Mladjenovic explained to her American audience: "The gun is no longer in the cellar or the closet, it is now visible so that it can be used by the man in the home as an instrument of intimidation."

While too few of the designers, funders, and administrators of DDR explicitly thought through what the politics of masculinity means for their actions, feminist activists and organizational workers have realized that most of these DDR planners implicitly take for granted that DDR is about men and boys. That is, they have planned and carried out their programs as if all the people they will be dealing with in DDR camps would be men. What they avoid is taking seriously in their operations the workings of ideas about manliness.

Feminist researchers, by contrast, working closely with local women's groups in conflict regions such as Uganda, Sierra Leone, Sri Lanka, Mozambique, and Liberia, have had gender questions in the front of their minds (Cohn 2013; Mazurana, Jacobsen, and Gale 2013). For instance, feminists have become wary of the vague term "child soldiers." The concept of the "child soldier"—and the reality it represents—has indeed aroused a new concern about children as young as eight being recruited, often forcibly, into armies. Nor have "child soldiers" been only those third-world boys and girls who capture media attention because they are sent into conflict operations. The practice of turning children into soldiers, many activists contend, should include the more widely adopted and seemingly more benign government policy of authorizing, promoting, and funding voluntary school-age cadet corps (New Profile 2004).

A new public consciousness was created through global campaigning by the Coalition to Stop the Use of Child Soldiers. Founded in 1998 by Amnesty International, Human Rights Watch, the Quakers, the Jesuit Refugee Service, and several other organizations, the Coalition to Stop the Use of Child Soldiers helped mobilize international support for ratifying and implementing the UN Convention on the Rights of the Child, passed in 1989. By 1998, 117 governments had signed and ratified the historic convention (Singer 2006). Others, such as the British and the U.S. governments, have been reluctant to sign and ratify the convention because it might hamper their efforts to introduce military cadet programs in high schools.

It is not that feminist-informed researchers and international peace workers criticize the use of the popular term "child soldier," they just don't think it is adequate. If one is committed to demilitarizing children who have been recruited into armies, then, they have found, one must ask when and how gender matters in how those children have experienced soldiering. So these feminist-informed researchers and practitioners have asked, "Where are the girls?" (McKay and Mazurana 2004). And following up on this innovative question, researchers discovered that girls have been recruited or coerced into fighting forces by all armed groups in a conflict and have been used by male commanders as porters, cooks, nurses, fighters, and sexual slaves (sometimes erroneously called "wives").

Moreover, these feminist researchers discovered that very few of these girls were receiving care from international or local organizations engaged in peacekeeping and national reconstruction. For instance, many of the agencies administering DDR camps made the handing in of a rifle the "ticket" for admission into the demobilization camps and the healthcare, job training, education, and psychological counseling those camps offered. But in most fighting forces, girls, while they played important roles in sustaining those forces, were only rarely issued guns. To make the DDR services accessible to girls trying to remake their lives after being used by fighting forces, the gun criterion would have to be eliminated. Furthermore, once one starts asking "Where are the girls?" one has to appropriate a lot more funding for the sort of post-traumatic stress syndrome care designed for girls who have endured sexual abuse, and a lot more resources for girls who, while still only sixteen or seventeen years old themselves, have come out of the fighting forces with small children of their own as a result of having been used as older male commanders' "wives." "Girl-headed household" would have to be a concept used by any policymaker who hoped to implement a realistic and meaningful postwar peacekeeping and reconstruction program (Fox 2004; Krosch 2005; McKay and Mazurana 2004).

In 2000, a first-of-its-kind international policy decision was made that today is making it sound less "odd" and more "reasonable" to ask "What about masculinity?" and "Where are the girls?" In October 2000, the fifteen delegates to the UN Security Council passed "Resolution 1325 on Women, Peace and Security." For the first time in its fifty-five years, the UN Security Council had passed a resolution specifically addressing the condition of women. Resolution 1325 called on all UN agencies and the officials of all of the 193 UN member states to do two things they had neglected or resisted.

First, Security Council Resolution 1325 called on both staff members of all UN agencies, as well as officials of all UN member governments, to pay explicit attention to the conditions and experiences and needs of women and girls in war zones. No longer, according to Resolution 1325, could rapes of women—by anyone—be swept under the rug or dismissed as merely an allegedly natural phenomenon of war. No longer could "refugees" be planned for and administered as if distributing food rations through men as alleged "heads of households" had the same political consequences as distributing those supplies through women. No longer could "child soldiers" be treated as if girls and boys in a fighting force had had the identical experiences—and thus had the same post-conflict traumas or socioeconomic prospects.

Second, Resolution 1325 called on UN agencies and governments to make sure that women, especially in local women's advocacy organizations, had a voice in decision-making at every step of the peace process. No longer should the negotiations to craft the conditions for a cease-fire among the warring groups be an all-male affair. No longer should women be left out of the closed-door decision-making processes that constructed the new militaries, new police forces, new courts, new legislatures, and new executives. No longer should new post-conflict constitutions be drafted by male-dominated assemblies. No longer should international and local male officials and leaders feel satisfied when they had considered women as mere victims. Under Resolution 1325, women, including those victimized by the warring parties, should be treated as political players.

Like the Mine Ban Treaty, the Geneva Conventions, the Convention against Torture, the Convention on the Rights of the Child, and the new Arms Trade Treaty, Security Council Resolution 1325 is an agreement that ultimately has to be implemented by specific governments and international agencies. Yet Resolution 1325 also owes its ideas to non-governmental activists and its passage to the pressure applied by those groups, who finally persuaded the governmental delegates to pass it. In the story of the passage of Resolution 1325, the intellectual and strategic roles played by the women of the Women's International League for Peace and Freedom (WILPF) who worked in the New York office across the street from the UN were crucial (Cohn 2013; Hill, Aboitiz, and Poehlman-Doumbouya 2003; Hill, Cohn, and Enloe 2006; Pratt and Richter-Devroe 2011).

Among the less-anticipated consequences of the passage of—and interpretation and attempted application of—Resolution 1325 has been the shining of a bright light on the gender dynamics inside the international peacekeeping operations themselves. When more people began to take seriously the experiences, ideas, and organizational priorities of women and women's organizations in societies to which the United Nations and NATO were sending peacekeeping and reconstruction teams, they began to ask fresh questions about whether the international civilian aid providers and military peacekeepers themselves might be having a less-than-positive impact on local women's and girls' lives. This meant taking stock of the masculinized and racialized biases among "the good guys." Many people used to seeing themselves as the rational, well-meaning, civilized, altruistic actors were, not surprisingly, uncomfortable under this new scrutiny.

"Peacekeepers" suddenly could be seen as men—men with particular, often diverse notions of what it meant to be deployed as a soldier on a peacekeeping mission. That is, their own notions of masculinity were revealed as a significant factor in how they conducted their militarized peacekeeping operations. Women and girls in Cambodia, East Timor, Bosnia, Kosovo, Liberia, and the Central African Republic would have to figure out ways to cope with—and organize and strategize to confront—those notions and the men's behaviors that flowed from them. And local women in societies coming out of militarized conflict would have to confront men in international peacekeeping forces at the same time as they sought to challenge abusive behavior and arrogance of men in their own communities—men who often acted out their own sense of frustration, anger, and confusion with violence toward women in their households, communities, and refugee camps (Cockburn and Zarkov 2002; Joshi 2005; www.aidsfreeworld.org).

When international aid workers, peacekeeping officials, and government and private foundation donors assumed that reaching out to "local leaders" meant working with the men who had influential positions in the post-conflict societies—leaders of villages, town mayors, heads of political parties, clerical authorities—then the patriarchal hurdles that local women activists confronted in trying to have a voice in peacemaking and national reconstruction loomed even higher: those male "local leaders" were often no less scornful of women's policy ideas than the international officials reaching out to them. That is, "local leaders," when left ungendered, is not in itself a guarantee of the sort of representation that can move a society effectively toward sustainable demilitarization.

Many male soldiers chosen by their home governments for deployment on UN or NATO peacekeeping missions still attach the highest value to combat. The appeal of combat is why they joined the military. Combat experience is what would earn them the greatest respect (and maybe promotion and extra pay) from their military comrades and superiors and from their fellow citizens back home. Combat is what they had been trained for. Combat would earn them the sought-after status of "real men" (Whitworth 2004).

Further undermining many peacekeeping soldiers' ability to engage in effective peace building are their stereotypes about the women and the men in the country to which they are deployed—the women as needing their superior protection, the men as not being capable of protecting their women. They exchange needed food for a "date," not thinking of it as having anything to do with prostitution, but feeling that they, the manly men, are doing a good deed (Higate and Henry 2004; Kronsell 2012).

Because serious consideration about the interplay of demilitarizing policies and the politics of militarized masculinity was not "on the agenda" prior to the passage of Resolution 1325 and only barely given the nod after its formal passage, peacekeeping has been experienced by many women as prostitution, sex trafficking, and sexual harassment (Bolkovac 2011; Refugees International 2005).

So much of this new global feminist-informed thinking about demilitarization—what it is, what undermines it, how it can be achieved and sustained—hinges on revising our ideas about security. Security turns out to be a broad, many-layered goal. It can no longer be imagined as simply synonymous with militarized security. Security, many women activists working to end armed conflict in various countries have concluded, has to be seen more realistically and more broadly, and that means it has to be seen as more complicated (Jacobson 2005). Security is one of the goals of demilitarization because so many people have discovered that militarization—that is, coming to see the world as dangerous, learning to be preoccupied with enemies, bolstering executive power in the name of fighting those enemies, starting to define one's patriotism and the criteria for belonging according to military service, or deferring to those who have done military service—has caused them to feel less, not more, secure. Security for many women and girls also comes, more are beginning to realize, less from fortifying the country's borders or driving out of their towns people of other ethnic groups than from finding ways to escape violent assaults perpetrated by men in their own homes.

Yet the familiar militarized ways of conceptualizing security remain stubbornly entrenched.

Listen to Nadine Puechguirbal. She is a French woman with years of experience on UN peacekeeping missions in Congo and Haiti. Her recent job was as "gender advisor" to the UN peacekeeping mission in Haiti, a post created by the UN to carry out its new responsibilities under Resolution 1325. Nadine Puechguirbal discovered, though, that neither the international military nor the police units deployed to bring peace to the Haitian people—a people who had endured years of dictatorship, partisan gang warfare, and a succession of devastating hurricanes and floods—were ready to expand their conventional ideas about creating security. Nor did these experts want to take seriously the ideas of the local Haitian feminists—women whom she had found to be practical, knowledgeable, and committed.

She summarized the typical reply of those male peacekeeping military officers who resisted her attempts to bring these Haitian women activists to the planning table: "They don't need to participate in the decision-making process because we can do this for them." And if this familiar assertion that women are merely victims, not decision makers, seemed wobbly, then the international officials fell back on claims of urgency: "It's an emergency, we have no time for gender, we'll add that later." The results?

- Women became the recipients of the internationally distributed food, but only the distribution points were staffed with peacekeepers, and on the long walks home, over the hills, women were attacked by armed male gangs who stole their precious supplies.
- International administrators of Haiti's peacekeeping era elections thought of security in conventional terms, deploying military peacekeepers only around the polling stations, without considering the more realistic ways in which Haitian women strategized about security; thus when election day came, many women did

not walk the miles to the nearest polling station both because they could not trust that their children would be safe while they were away for hours and because they realistically feared they would be attacked on the long walk to vote (Enloe 2013; Puechguirbal 2003, 2006).

While the U.S. government's delegate voted for Resolution 1325 (it is a resolution, not a treaty, and thus does not require signing and ratification), the resolution—its analytical premises, its requirements—is virtually unknown among Americans. Neither U.S. officials nor any reporters covering American military or civilian policies and practices in Afghanistan or Iraq ever mention Resolution 1325. That does not mean that Afghan and Iraqi activist women haven't heard about Resolution 1325. One of the strategies of the WILPF and other supporters of the ground-breaking Security Council resolution was to immediately distribute the text of Resolution 1325 to as many local women's groups around the world as possible—that is, to globalize Resolution 1325 in order to give local activists a sense of empowerment and to provide them with a lever to open up the still-masculinized political processes in their own war-torn or post-conflict societies. This transnational feminist campaign to globalize 1325 continues today by trying to get individual governments to "own" it, that is, to pass their own "National Action Plans" for its implementation (www.peacewomen.org).

In Afghanistan one of the principal critiques articulated by local Afghan women's groups is that the U.S. occupying forces and their superiors in Washington depended heavily on the male commanders of the regional militias (referred to as the Northern Alliance) in their military invasion to topple the Taliban regime, without taking into account how militarized and patriarchal those commanders were. Consequently, now, with the new constitutional system's legislature and president (and his cabinet) struggling to exert their civilian authority, those conservative militarized commanders (often called "warlords") remain entrenched in positions of power as governors, police chiefs, and the dominant bloc in the newly elected legislature. One member of the new legislature, Malai Joya, a twenty-seven-year-old woman already active in a local women's organization, won a seat in the 2005 national elections. What made her famous among Afghans was her standing up in the new legislature in December 2005 to denounce those male legislators who were "criminal warlords . . . whose hands are stained with the blood of the people" (Coghan 2006; Coleman and Hunt 2006). In the wake of her public denunciation of the patriarchal and militarized warlords, principal players in the anti-Taliban Northern Alliance, Malai Joya was subjected to death threats.

What Malai Joya underscored in her dramatic speech was what Resolution 1325 also implies: demilitarization cannot be achieved unless women are empowered to the point that all the forms of masculinized militarization are exposed and rolled back. Most of those local and international officials determining how peace building and post-conflict reconstruction will proceed do not think in these terms. In their planning for the U.S.-led invasion and occupation of Afghanistan, American officials did not think deeply about the causes of militarization or about what it would take to reverse it; they made forming alliances with the existing anti-Taliban warlords a priority. The ramifications of that U.S. decision continue to be felt in the lives of Afghan women and men (Enloe 2004).

In October 2015, thousands of feminist peace activists from dozens of countries converged on New York to mark the fifteenth anniversary of the UN's passage of 1325. They were not, however, in a celebratory mood. They held panels and press conferences at the UN headquarters and all over the city to spell out the failures of 1325's implementation. Women still were not taken seriously in most peace negotiations nor were they involved in the political and economic decision-making that was shaping post-war societies (Chang et al. 2015).

As if to confirm these women's assertions, an interstate meeting was convened in Vienna two weeks later to search for a peace formula that would end the escalating war in Syria. The official photo shows the seventeen invited states' delegates seated at long tables facing each other, with their countries' flags providing a backdrop behind the head table. Every single person in the photo is male.

Demilitarization efforts in so many countries—both developed and developing, both war-torn and war-waging—have been resisted by those individuals and groups who have realized that pushing a demilitarization process beyond tokenism would require dismantling patriarchal structures, not only in the public realm, but in the private sphere as well. Genuine, lasting, and thoroughgoing demilitarization, in other words, would necessitate transforming relationships between women and women, between women and men, between men and men, and between women and men and all the influential institutions of society—schools, legislatures, religious organizations, corporations, the media, the military, the offices of prime ministers and presidents.

Sustainable demilitarization requires changing the relationships between masculinized authority figures and feminized "dependents," awarding the education department as much political influence as the defense department, and withdrawing from male citizens—especially those claiming insider military knowledge—their privileged status as the citizens presumed to be "expert" on security issues.

CHAPTER 8

THE GLOBALIZED LIVES OF JAPANESE WOMEN

Globalizing Insights from Local Japanese Places

We still do not fully understand exactly how and why militarization—or its reversal—"works." What makes a middle-aged man look back on his years in the military as "the best years of my life"? What makes a young woman travel far from home to Syria to marry a male fighter? What makes an engineer take special pride in helping to design a weapons system?

But we have learned that if we watch militarization as a process—something that happens over time to real people in big and little steps—we are likely to be more subtle and realistic in our understanding. If we are more subtly realistic in how we explain militarization, then our recommendations for how to reverse it will be more effective. To be *subtly realistic*—that is our analytical goal. To get there we will need to be curious about how militarization happens, not just to men, not just to governments or to soldiers, not just to companies or political parties or universities, but to diverse women in their everyday ("unimportant," "trivial," "private") lives.

In this spirit of careful, subtle gender inquiry, it is valuable to look and listen to Japanese women today. Japan's citizens are being today urged by some of their leading policymakers to militarize, in the name of staving off China's military expansionism, of becoming a "mature" state, and of asserting more influence on the global stage. Only by wielding its military might, these current leaders insist, will Japan be deemed worthy (in the eyes of other militarily strong states) of gaining a seat on the UN Security Council.

In the midst of these pressures, each Japanese woman and man has to decide if this argument makes sense. Will accepting this argument give her or him a greater sense of genuine security?

The constitution of Japan, written in 1947 under the U.S. postwar occupation authority, includes an article that is rare among the world's constitutions. Most Japanese simply refer to it as "Article 9." It reads: "Aspiring sincerely to an international peace based on justice and order, the Japanese people forever renounce war as a sovereign right of the nation and the threat or use of force as means of settling international disputes."

In order to guarantee this, Article 9's writers continued: "Land, sea and air forces as well as other war potential, will never be maintained. The right of belligerency of the state will not be recognized" (Fellowship of Reconciliation 2005).

The American government, using its occupation authority during the late 1940s, pressured the Japanese to include this innovative article in their postwar constitution. Nevertheless, within less than a decade, while many Japanese had begun to see Article 9 as integral to their own sense of post-war national identity, many American officials had begun to exert pressure on their Japanese counterparts to commit themselves to diluting Article 9.

Once the horrors of World War II had faded and had become replaced in Washington by anxieties over the tensions of the U.S.-USSR globalized rivalry, American officials looked to Japan to serve as an ally—as a militarized ally—against both the Soviet Union and China, each defined as Communist threats to U.S. national security. Beginning in 1950 and still today, U.S. officials of both political parties have pressured the Japanese government to create a formidable modernized military, to allow the

United States to base naval, marine, and air force offensive units on its soil (especially on its southernmost island of Okinawa), to contribute Japanese taxpayers' yen to maintaining those U.S. bases, to participate in joint military maneuvers in Asia, and more recently to contribute military forces, albeit in carefully defined "noncombat" roles, to the U.S. military occupation of Iraq (Johnson 2003; Vine 2015).

Today, Article 9 still stands, but many Japanese fear for its survival. For many of these worried Japanese, most of whom have grown up in the era after World War II, Article 9 is central to their understanding of what it means to be Japanese in a globalized world. Article 9's pledge guarantees that Japan will play its international roles economically, politically, and culturally without relying on military might, thus making Japan a country that has the potential for developing broad global respect and trust.

For other Japanese, however, Article 9 is imagined to be the embodiment of humiliation. To them, it is a reminder of Japan's war-time defeat, surrender, and transformation at the hands of foreign occupiers. Article 9, in their eyes, hamstrings their country's ability to play the influential international leadership role it should, given its impressive economic achievements at home and abroad. A country that has created Sony, Mitsubishi, Honda, and Toyota, they believe, should be able to possess unfettered military might to complement its corporate might. These pro-militarization Japanese remain a minority but are growing in numbers and in political and popular influence. They argue that a "normal" country is one equipped with a full-fledged military and a pride in its own history. They applaud the government's recent decision to move the Self Defense Forces director out from under the prime minister's office and to a cabinet office of his own. They call for public singing of the national anthem in schools and at public events and showing the red-sun flag in schools and public places, practices until recently frowned upon by most Japanese. They want to require antimilitarist teachers to use textbooks that play down the Imperial Japanese Army's atrocities in World War II. They tend to support the right wing of the long-ruling electoral party, the Liberal Democratic Party (LDP). Thus, as in most countries, the debates about the costs and rewards of choosing militarization over demilitarization get played out in the arena of political party contests (Onishi 2006).

If they feel passionately about the need to eliminate Article 9, some Japanese may support the most outspoken nationalists, the men with bullhorns who shout their nationalist slogans outside Tokyo's busy shopping centers and subway stations. These vocal nationalists call on their compatriots first, to "get over" their collective guilt from World War II and second, to support the buildup of the country's military power in order to confront the forces of North Korea and China. They brush aside the anxieties expressed by their other Asian neighbors, many of whom still remember the horrors of occupation by the imperial Japanese forces in the 1930s and 1940s (Onishi 2006). Currently, Japan's prime minister Shinzo Abe, leader of the Liberal Democratic Party, echoes these nationalists' arguments.

For many Japanese today, however, Article 9 remains a source of both pride and security. They see this innovative constitutional provision as evidence that Japan will not revert to its earlier ways, which they interpret as having been imperial, colonizing, nationalist, and militaristic. They prefer to see the defeat in World War II as the source of important lessons—lessons that, if learned, will allow Japan to play a leading role globally as a model of how a country and its people can pursue prosperity without relying on authoritarianism and militarization. These Japanese worry about the apparent present-day marriage of convenience between the emerging Japanese nationalist, militarizing political right wing on the one side and on the other, those in Washington pressuring Japan to remilitarize.

Among these critics of Japanese remilitarization are Japanese feminists. While conservative nationalists have argued that guilt over past wars is debilitating and that building and deploying a military force is the avenue for taking Japan's rightful place in global affairs, Japanese feminists have been pursuing quite a different path toward globalized participation. After having launched new historical research, they are now acknowledging their uncomfortable finding: during the 1930s and early 1940s many ordinary Japanese women embraced a militarized version of nationalism, actively supporting their government's wars as housewives, mothers, wives of soldiers, city workers, farmers, and community organizers (Ueno 2004). This acknowledgment has not been easy.

Hundreds of Japanese women activists traveled to take part in the UN-sponsored international meetings marking the Decade of Women (1975–1985); even more Japanese women attended the historic UN-sponsored Beijing Conference on Women in 1995; and at least four hundred Japanese women—more than from any other country—traveled to New York in 2000 to take part in the "Beijing Plus Five" UN conference called to monitor the implementation of the Beijing Platform for Action signed by scores of governments in 1995, pledging them each to take steps to empower women. In addition, many Japanese women have been working in development aid projects from Uganda to Afghanistan and participating in dozens of smaller efforts organized with women from other Asian countries. With these actions, Japanese women's advocates have presented to their fellow citizens an alternative model of globalization—an alternative based on the argument that building trust through cooperation among equals holds out a better prospect for ensuring security than does nationalism-fueled militarization (Chan-Tiberghien 2004; Ueno 2004).

In December 2000, Japanese feminists active in a group called Violence Against Women Worldwide Network (VAWW NET) organized an international conference in the form of a women's tribunal to hear testimonies of women from around Asia—Korea, China, the Philippines, Taiwan, Indonesia, Singapore—who had been coerced during World War II into sexually servicing the male soldiers of the Imperial Japanese Army. They had several goals. First, they wanted to shine direct light on their own government's and their fellow citizens' untenable denial of this wartime sexual slavery practiced in their name. One group of these feminists created a small Tokyo museum devoted to making visible the experiences of those women—Korean, Filipino, Taiwanese, Indonesian, Singaporean—who were forcibly enlisted into the Japanese Imperial Army's brothel system. They call their museum Women's Active Museum on War and Peace (Henson 1999; www.wam-peace.org).

Second, these Japanese anti-militarism feminists wanted to build new alliances of trust and cooperation with women's advocates in other Asian countries—alliances that had continued to be hampered by many Asians' painful memories of previous Japanese conquest and imperialism. Europeans and North Americans often lump together women of such diverse countries as North and South Korea, China, Japan, Vietnam, Taiwan, Cambodia, Laos, Indonesia, Thailand, the Philippines, and Burma (renamed Myanmar by the military dictatorship) as merely "Asian." But being seen by Westerners as "Asian women" does not in reality guarantee shared memories, common understandings, or identical goals. Even launching a new journal published in Korea and titling it the *Asian Journal of Women's Studies* was subject to debate among the feminist scholars at the journal's home campus, Ehwa Women's University. After all, who was "Asian"? Were there any significant shared experiences and identities among Burmese, Japanese, and Korean women?

The VAWW NET's 2000 tribunal, therefore, was both risky and innovative. It drew scores of participants and provoked new awareness and fresh conversations about what happened during World War II and what sweeping away the denials of those events might do to turn a new page in relations among women of the region. But the organizers were dismayed when, under pressure from conservative government officials, NHK, the major Japanese television network, backed down from showing a documentary film about the tribunal. On the one hand, for many Japanese feminists this provided another piece of evidence of the growing influence of militarizing nationalists in their country's political life. On the other hand, they were heartened that they were offered support in challenging NHK by a trans-Asian feminist coalition called the Asia Pacific Forum on Women, Law and Development, which is based in Thailand. Its support suggested that the VAWW NET activists' second goal, to build new relationships of trust between Japanese feminists and women's advocates throughout Asia, was coming within reach (Kashiwazaki 2006).

The debate going on among Japanese today—and the significant role of the United States in influencing that debate, as well as the stakes the people of China, Taiwan, Indonesia, and Korea have in the outcomes of this debate—makes it crucial that we understand the diverse ways in which Japanese women experience militarization and resistance to militarization. Moreover, the debates that Japanese women are engaging in today resonate in many countries. Japanese women and men are not alone in being encouraged

- to interpret their country's constitution in ways that make it easier for the executive branch to deploy the military;
- to teach children that the country's past is unblemished; and
- to define a "normal country" as one with a potent military force.

I had the chance to visit Okinawa in March 2003. Okinawa once was an independent kingdom but was conquered by Japan. It was as a province of Japan that Okinawa was invaded by the large U.S. military force in 1945 as part of a strategy for defeating the Japanese and ending World War II. The March to June 1945 Battle of Okinawa was one of the most devastating battles of the war. For the next thirty years, the U.S. government ruled as the occupying authority in Okinawa, even after the rest of Japan was returned to sovereignty. These were the years of the Cold War. American military strategists came to value Okinawa as a major military base. Many of its marines and pilots deployed to Vietnam were stationed in Okinawa. In 1972, under pressure from a reviving Japan, the United States returned Okinawa to Japanese rule, but with the important proviso that the United States would be allowed to continue to use hundreds of acres of valuable farm and coastal lands in Okinawa for its military bases. In fact, two-thirds of all the thousands of U.S. troops now stationed in Japan are stationed on its small southern island. This arrangement between the two governments has inspired neither trust nor gratitude among many Okinawans toward officials in Tokyo or their counterparts in Washington (Taira 2003).Yet most Americans would have a hard time finding Okinawa on a world map, much less describing its complex political place in global militarized politics. Thus, my own brief visit to Okinawa in 2003 was a chance to be tutored.

There were five of us from mainland Japan (I was then a visiting professor in Tokyo) who were hosted by Suzuyo Takazato and other Okinawan women active in the group Okinawa Women Act Against Military Violence (OWAAMV). The visit was eye-opening.

On the last day Kaori Hirouchi was seeing off a mainland Japanese colleague, Amane Funabashi, and me at Okinawa's main airport. Kaori brought her little seven-month-old baby with her to the airport. When she saw me, she exclaimed, "Look at what a friend just gave me!" As women always do for their friends with new babies, several of Kaori's friends had passed along used baby clothes. The exchange of used baby clothes is one of those economies only a feminist might notice. Kaori said, "Look at this." She pulled out a pair of cute little baby socks. Her friend in Okinawa had given her these socks because they would fit her new little son beautifully. The miniature cotton socks were khaki and were decorated with images of little bomber airplanes. Standing there in the airport, Kaori holding the baby socks in her hand as one would a piece of valuable evidence, the three of us began wondering together: What did her friend think of as "cute"? Can one militarize "cuteness"? Can one militarize the friendships between women as mothers?

Our feminist curiosities were sparking now. Would her generous friend have thought it appropriate to pass along to Kaori these same hand-me-down bomber-decorated socks if her baby were a girl? Does living as a woman in Okinawa, where the operations of U.S. military bases weave in and out of civilian daily life, make bombers seem as ordinary or as "cute" as a toy fire truck or a panda bear?

Baby socks. If we activate our feminist curiosity, we can plumb deeper into the subtleties of feminized militarization—how and why motherhood can (never automatically) become militarized; how the most seemingly harmless of fashions can (again, never automatically) become militarized; how friendship between women can sometimes become militarized. Baby socks? Lacking a feminist curiosity, baby socks will appear trivial—that is, not worth paying attention to in one's search for causes. It requires an active feminist curiosity to treat these seemingly "nonpolitical" events with analytical seriousness, to understand their causal potency.

On our first day in Okinawa, we mainlanders were taken around the main island by Keiko Itokazu, a woman who had become an active member of OWAAMV and, more recently, an elected member of the Okinawa prefecture legislature. She took us to World War II memorials, to museums, to the famous caves. And as we drove in the car from place to place, Keiko Itokazu pointed out open fields and fenced-off areas, telling us their political histories. Keiko Itokazu describes her profession as that of a "peace guide." Suddenly, I realized, "Oh, all the other guides are not." But Keiko Itokazu hadn't always been a "peace guide." That is a profession she has helped create on Okinawa. She began her career in Okinawa's "second industry," tourism, as a tour-bus guide. Up in front of the bus, microphone in hand, Keiko would give visiting tourists, most of them sun seekers from chilly mainland Japan, the conventional rendition of Okinawan history, offering her listeners a historical vision of heroism and sacrifice during the horrific Battle of Okinawa. Over the miles in between these featured sites, she would give her voice a rest, finding little of interest to talk about as the rural Okinawan landscape passed by.

Several years ago, however, a group of Okinawan peace activists invited the local tour-bus guides to meet for a conversation. It was a challenging conversation. The peace activists asked Keiko and her fellow guides: "Do you realize that in the way you're practicing your own profession you are helping to militarize memories—Okinawans' memories, tourists' memories? Do you realize that by saying nothing about lost arable land, about what all these miles of fences mean, you are militarizing every visitor's understanding of the landscape and making the conversion of vegetable farms into military runways seem normal?" The peace activists pressed each of their fellow Okinawans working as tour-bus guides to assign more serious meaning to their seemingly "trivial" occupation, to see for the first time the deep implications of what they said up in the front of their tour buses—and what each chose to leave unsaid.

Not all of the tour guides who participated in this uncomfortable conversation decided to transform their profession—to take steps to demilitarize tour guiding. But Keiko Itokazu did. She could only demilitarize her profession, however, if she, working with women in OWAAMV, could figure out what exactly was militarized in her previous script and what was militarized in her previous silences.

This might be a good point at which to remind ourselves what it means for a person, an occupation, a relationship, a town, an industry, or a memory to become militarized. First, anything is on its way to becoming militarized if it is increasingly coming under the control of a military—of a military's rules, its budget, its command structure. Second, and perhaps harder to chart, anything is becoming militarized if it is increasingly (more than last year, more than a generation ago) dependent on militaristic ideas, concepts, or values for its safety, its sense of self-worth, its status of belonging, its economic well-being, its social legitimacy, even its alleged "normalcy." As we have seen, women and men do not become militarized in identical ways. Furthermore, almost anything—a town, a school, a company, a museum, a legislature, a ministry—becomes militarized in significant part due to someone's manipulations of ideas about femininity and ideas about masculinity.

Now let's look at what it has taken for a particular Japanese woman to resist these subtle everyday workings of militarization. We had to travel to Kyushu, one of Japan's three major islands, south of Honshu (where Tokyo is located), but north of Okinawa. When I visited Kyushu, it was February. The mud was soggy and the air cold. Only a few brave plum trees so far had dared to bloom. A former graduate student and now a globally minded feminist, Yukiko Oda, introduced me to Hiroko Watanabe. Yukiko Oda and I spent an afternoon and evening with Hiroko Watanabe, learning how she had become committed not only to resisting her own militarization but also to making visible the minute ways in which her Kyushu neighbors were being sucked, step by step, into the process of militarization.

Hiroko Watanabe was a dairy farmer. Dressed in blue jeans and muddy sneakers, her hair cut short, Hiroko exuded a sense of purpose—actually, a sense of multiple interlocking purposes. Hiroko was determined to sustain her small dairy business, an occupation that she believes provides life-giving food, despite the ups and downs of government and industry pricing.

At the same time, Hiroko Watanabe was determined not to surrender to the pressures on her to become passively resigned to the expansion of the Japan Self-Defense Forces (SDF) base in her town of Tsuiki. She walked us around the fenced perimeter of the SDF base. She pointed out the F-16 fighter planes parked on the runway. She made sure that we looked at the decorative bushes at our elbows, planted just outside the base fence and paid for by the SDF—as a gesture of "neighborliness." Or was it an effort at cooptation? You can militarize a dairy farmer. You can militarize a flowering bush. She showed us the main gate to the base where on the second day of every month, for over a decade, Hiroko Watanabe and anyone else who was moved to join her come to sit with banners calling for respect for Article 9 of Japan's "peace" constitution.

Hiroko Watanabe got up at five o'clock every morning. From six to ten, she milked her cows and cleaned out their stalls. From five to nine every night, Hiroko did her second four-hour shift, returning to the barn to milk the other half of her cow herd and clean out their stalls. Cows are tyrants. If you are a dairy farmer, you cannot ever leave your cows. So resisting your own militarization and the militarization of your fellow townspeople has to be done in the few hours between your shifts with the cows.

Over tea in her home, Hiroko told Yukiko Oda and me of the constant pressures on citizens of Tsuiki and of the three other towns whose land the SDF controlled: pressures to accept Tokyo money, pressures to accept Tokyo-designed construction projects, pressures to hand over more land for air force runways, and pressures to give up any sense that their elected diet and local council representatives can shape military policy. When the men in these elected posts spoke of the SDF's impact on their towns, they spoke, Hiroko explained, in the tones of "rationality."

To be rational, after all, is to be masculine. To be masculine is to be rational. Even a woman trying to break into the masculinized world of Japanese electoral politics must adopt this "rational" stance if she wants to be taken seriously in the masculinized halls of government. But what if this sort of masculinized rationality is really only a camouflaged version of political resignation? What if this "rationality" is a means for elected officials to accept the imposed militarization without appearing helpless and thus feminized?

Hiroko Watanabe refused to measure her own rationality in these masculinized terms. Instead, she—in between her daily morning and evening milkings and barn cleanings—published a newsletter to make visible the typically ignored minutiae of local militarization. In doing so, in refusing to adopt a masculinized form of resignation, Hiroko risked being labeled "unrealistic" and "naive"—in other words, "feminine."

Baby socks. Motherhood. Friendship. Tourism. Bus guides. Memory. Milking cows. Construction projects. Femininity. Town councilors. Rationality. Masculinity. Civilian resignation.

The things that seem to need to be militarized for the sake of implementing and legitimizing a militarized national security policy are far more numerous and diverse—and often far from the inner sanctum of political elites—than we usually imagine. And the workings of gender together with the lives of women weave in and out of every one of them.

Only by exercising a feminist curiosity—only by taking seriously the exploration of women's daily experiences and often trivialized ideas—are we likely to discover the appropriate explanatory weight that each of these deserves. While femininity is almost always manipulated (rewarded, nurtured, taught, discouraged, punished, avoided) in the process of militarizing national security, femininity comes in more than one form. We are realizing, thanks to all the cross-cultural, cross-class, cross-generational women's studies investigations, that there are myriad femininities. Thus, to realistically explore how the processes of gendering militarization both rely on and serve to shape ideas and practices of both masculinity and femininity, we will have to keep our curiosity open to diverse femininities being militarized separately but often simultaneously.

Take, for instance, an imagined woman we will call "Angelina." She is a white American woman in her mid-thirties married to an officer in the marines who is still in the early stages of his military career. He has just been assigned to a U.S. base in Okinawa. Angelina is nervous about being so far away from her family and friends in her home state of Florida. But she is relieved that she has at least been able to go with her husband to this Okinawa posting. She's been so lonely when he's been deployed overseas for months at a time. Angelina is just getting settled on the base in Okinawa and is pleased because the military family apartment she has been assigned at Camp Foster is so much better than the housing that she and her husband had on the military base back in North Carolina. She's heard from other marines' wives that this is because these U.S. base apartments are paid for by the Tokyo government. Plus, she thinks there are such great recreation facilities on this base for her two children. So here is Angelina living in Okinawa as an American military wife. She is far away from friends and has given up the chance to have a career of her own. But for now, she reasons, there are at least the warm breezes of Okinawa and the marine housing facilities at Camp Foster to enjoy.

At the same time, to the north in Tokyo, an imagined Japanese woman, "Yoko," is busy strategizing about her own career in what she has come to see as the thoroughly masculinized world of Japanese international journalism. Yoko is in her late twenties. She does not want to be a decorative feminine presence serving as an anchor on the evening news. Instead, Yoko wants to be sent overseas to cover real news. She wants to break into the men's world of foreign correspondents. There are wars being waged in the Middle East. Yoko has persuaded her senior editor to let her join the team from a major national newspaper, the *Asahi Shimbun*, that is being sent to cover the war in Syria. This is a breakthrough. Perhaps Yoko will be the first woman reporter in the history of the *Asahi Shimbun* assigned by this still-male-dominated prestigious newspaper to cover a war. Yoko is not a warmonger. She is personally opposed to the government's Liberal Democratic Party–controlled cabinet's support of the U.S. administration's war policy. But, she thinks to herself, this war may offer her a great career opportunity. War is where so many male journalists have made their reputations. So Yoko is packing her bag; she is on her way to Syria. She will prove to her editor, to her male colleagues, and to the Japanese newspaper readers (just as American and European women reporters have tried to prove) that a woman can do a "man's job"—cover a war (www.nojobforawoman .com).

Now let's turn our attention again to the south, back to Okinawa. But this time let's pay serious attention to the life and thoughts of a woman whom we will call "Mrs. Miyagi." She defines her own femininity largely in terms of being a good wife. Her husband is a fisherman who fishes off the coast just north of Naha City. This is where Tokyo government officials and Washington government officials have agreed that the U.S. base further south will be relocated; the existing military base, Camp Schwab, will be expanded so that it can accommodate the military plane U.S. designers have named the "Osprey." Japanese officials thus approached Mrs. Miyagi's husband and pressured him to sell his fishing rights to the government so that it will be easier to consolidate this land for the military base without much local opposition from the people in and near Naha City. Mrs. Miyagi and her husband talked about it together. It was a big decision. They decided that there was not much choice; Camp Schwab was going to be expanded one way or another. Of the two, her husband was more resigned; he thought taking the Tokyo/Washington money was the most rational thing to do. But Mrs. Miyagi was hesitant. She had women friends in the coastal towns who were hanging banners, selling vegetables to raise funds, doing everything possible to stop Camp Schwab's expansion into their ecologically fragile bay. If she agreed with her husband to sell his fishing rights to the government, would she be letting down her friends?

Already we can see that there is not just one kind of femininity that is being militarized. The U.S.-fostered and the locally encouraged militarization of Japan require the militarizing transformations of the ideas, hopes, aspirations, fears, and work of diverse women—most of them Japanese. But some of those women who need to be militarized in order to ensure the militarization of Japan are American women.

Femininities are intersected with class, ethnic, generational, and national dynamics. Yet in each instance, it is a form of femininity that is being militarized. If we are not curious about the complex workings of femininity in particular women's lives, we will not be able to reliably explain why and how the subtle process of militarization occurs—or is reversed.

Also, as even just these three examples reveal, a variety of femininities are being manipulated to fuel militarization in not just one but several countries simultaneously. So today, in order to realistically explore efforts to remilitarize Japan, we need to look outside Japan, to the United States. Let's think about a woman we'll call "Cheryl." She is an African American woman, nineteen years old, and she has joined the U.S. Navy right out of high school because she has heard from both her older brother and her Chicago high school guidance counselor that you are less likely to experience racism in the U.S. military than in most American civilian workplaces. Furthermore, the navy recruiter tells Cheryl that, once she has enlisted, the navy will help her pay for a future college education. She is determined, somehow, to go to college. She is also aware that the U.S. economy is unpredictable; so many of her friends are having a hard time getting more than a minimum-wage job. So, overall, even though she doesn't imagine a world populated by enemies and knows that security takes forms that have little to do with submarines and rockets, Cheryl decides that joining the navy makes sense.

After finishing basic training, Cheryl is pleased when she is assigned to a supply ship that is soon due to sail to Yokohama. Her mother is worried. She has heard Washington officials sounding so eager to "wage war on terrorists." Cheryl's mother believes that if her government spent more on education and community-styled policing, there would be less crime and more security in her own Chicago neighborhood. But Cheryl assures her mother that serving on a supply ship, she will not be anywhere near combat; even if she is deployed to the Middle East, she will be offshore, not patrolling roads through insurgent neighborhoods. Moreover, Cheryl tells her still-skeptical mother, African Americans are more likely to gain full equality in American society if they prove that they are patriotic. And what is more patriotic than joining the U.S. Navy? Cheryl is one of the American sailors now living in Yokohama.

Consider now another American woman, "Susan." Her life is also about to become tied to the lives of Japanese women. She is a white, precariously middle-class woman living and selling real estate in a small city in upper New York State. She is in her fifties, divorced, and a single mother with two teenage sons. The younger boy is doing fine. He loves school, has an after-school job, and helps Susan with the laundry.

But Susan worries about her older son, Tom. He's been out of high school for almost a year. He just squeaked through to graduate. Now he hangs around the house all day, drinking Cokes, watching television, and playing war games on his computer. Susan feels she has failed as a mother. Maybe if Tom joined the marines, it would make a mature man out of her son. With this hope in mind, she decides to give him motherly encouragement when he shows signs of enthusiasm after seeing the enticing recruiting ads for the marines on television. If her son succeeds as a soldier, Susan thinks, she could feel like a successful mother. She worries about her son being deployed to Afghanistan, so she breathes a sigh of relief when Tom is sent to Okinawa. Neither Susan nor Tom has ever heard of Okinawa, but when they look on a map they can see it is far away from Afghanistan.

I had been trying out some of these ideas about how particular women thought about their own relationships to the military during a series of evening talks in Tokyo. I wondered what members of the audience thought. So during the evening I asked them—women and men—to do some of their own imagining and to stand up and "become" a woman whose femininity has been (willingly or unwillingly) militarized for the sake of perpetuating—or maybe questioning—the U.S.-Japan government-to-government international security alliance. There were lots of volunteers.

"I am a Filipino woman working near a U.S. military base in Okinawa," the first Japanese woman explained. She explained that (in this guise) she had immigrated to Japan by paying a hefty fee to an employment agency. She also explained that she grew up on one of the poorer islands of the Philippines and hoped to work as a respectable entertainer with a migrant worker's visa issued by the Japanese government. But now she found herself in Okinawa. Back home in the Philippines she had prepared for work abroad by learning a full repertoire of American rock 'n' roll and country and western songs. But now here in Okinawa she wasn't singing; she was working in a disco, trying to persuade male customers to buy her diluted "ladies' drinks" and supplying sexual services to young, bored American male marines in the decaying discos just outside the gates of Camp Hansen. She is afraid to tell her parents. Her mother is sure to be disappointed, seeing her as failing to live up to the standards of a respectable Catholic Filipino woman. Furthermore, she is barely making enough money to send home to her rural parents. Now that the yen-dollar exchange rate has left the American men with little spending money, some of her customers prefer the cheaper system of bringing women to their living quarters inside the base, thus avoiding the disco-owners' bar charges. Although this practice is allegedly a violation of the U.S. Marines' rules, no American officers seem to pay much attention when their soldiers bring civilian women onto the base for sex.

A man in the audience stands. "I am a female employee of a Japanese construction company. I work as a secretary," he explains as he adopts this role. "I'm forty-five years old. I could only find this part-time job. But it really helps cover the family's expenses because my husband's own full-time job with a big bank is so insecure. Some of his friends already have lost their corporate jobs. I know that the Liberal Democratic Party legislators and the national government tell local town councils that the government will build new roads, bridges, even sports centers, in return for the town's cooperation in voting to host an SDF or U.S. military base. I'm not sure that this is a good exchange for the local people. But we've been struggling through the drawn-out recession here in Japan and, in this still-fragile economy, I need to keep my clerical job. So I'm really relieved that my boss has developed such close relations with the ruling LDP and gets some of the lucrative construction contracts in the military-base towns. These government contracts make my own job a bit more secure."

A woman then stands. "I am a girl who has recently gotten a job as a civilian employee inside the U.S. Navy base at Yokohama because I want to be able to buy jeans more cheaply on base and can eat American food." This member of the audience is in her fifties, but she is trying to think like a twenty-one-year-old Japanese woman. She knows how seductive U.S. consumer culture is for many Japanese. "I can shop at the PX on the base and can eat at the McDonald's on the base for much less than at the McDonald's in Ikebukuro." Neither the cosmetics sold at a discount in the PX nor the "Chicken McNuggets" at McDonald's seem to this young Japanese woman to be remotely related to war, foreign policy, or violence. Furthermore, in her bookkeeping job on the base, she can improve her English: "Everyone knows that to get ahead today you need to be able to speak English. For a Japanese woman, I think that is especially valuable, don't you?"

It is worth pausing here for a moment to do an accounting of what has been militarized as a result of militarizing these women's—Japanese, Filipino, and American—feminized lives that are in different ways tied to Japan: daughterhood, marriage, motherhood, secretarial and bookkeeping jobs, learning English, fast food, education, patriotism, entertainment, sexuality, consumerism, economic security, and fashion. Militarizing femininities—in all their diversity—seems to be crucial for sustaining the Tokyo-Washington bilateral military security agreement. If one pays no attention to the politics of femininity in particular women's lives, it is likely that any political commentator will produce an unreliable analysis of the politics that today sustain the Japanese–U.S. alliance. This does not mean that women control the alliance. They clearly have little power in the often-tense alliance negotiations. But the male elites of both countries do rely upon a lot of women to think of their own feminized lives in ways that make militarization "normal" and thus almost invisible.

Now back to the audience. "I am an Okinawan woman who has trained as an actress," a woman in the back row tells us. "I have just gotten the chance I've been working for: I have been invited by a major Japanese film director to audition for a film set during World War II. I will play the female romantic lead, the fiancée of a brave Japanese pilot." She then explains that she knows from her mother and her Okinawan teachers that the Battle of Okinawa was not just a story of romance and bravery and that many Okinawans of her grandparents' generation paid a terrible price for being caught in the middle between the imperial and American forces in the spring of 1945. "But the film script is wonderful. And how often does an Okinawan actress get a chance to play the romantic lead in a mainland-produced film? I have to try out for it. And, after all, it's only a love story!"

At this point in our discussion, I wondered aloud what members of the audience thought were the reasons increasing numbers of young Japanese women were volunteering for the Japan Self-Defense Forces. Did their motivations have to do with the politics of femininity in contemporary Japan? As Japanese professor Fumika Sato has uncovered in her important research, Japanese civilian officials in charge of SDF planning, motivated by a desire to expand the country's military without diluting its quality, have raised the women's proportion of the SDF's soldiers to 5 percent, an all-time high. But that has been achieved only because many young women now have their own reasons for enlisting in the SDF.

At this point three women—of different ages—suddenly stood up. The first woman, in her sixties, imagined herself as a member of the SDF and, playing that role, told us: "I am single and twenty-six years old. I majored in mathematics at university and also in graduate school. I wanted to work for the SDF as an air traffic controller because it's a job that requires mathematical skills but is not open to young women at civilian airports." This contribution showed us that the militarization of a woman-as-mathematician is easier in any society that presumes that mathematics is a "naturally" masculinized profession. If this same Japanese twenty-six-year-old were male, therefore, he would have more opportunities open to him in the civilian air traffic controller profession, and thus it would be harder to militarize him. By contrast, the officials making personnel decisions for the SDF categorize "combat" jobs as the most masculine and thus today might tolerate some dilution of the masculinized culture in other job sectors of their military, for instance, in their own air force control towers.

Not all women who volunteer for the SDF, however, are motivated by identical aspirations. A second woman, also role-playing, explained: "I had just graduated from high school and was looking for a job. I saw a recruiting poster—all the people looked nice, they were smiling, there were no guns, and I thought the uniform was cool." This contribution makes us look again at the militarization of women's smiles and women's fashion. Fashion designers are always thinking about varieties of femininity. Some fashion designers work for militaries. Militaries all over the world think about the design of their uniforms so that they can appeal to men's sense of masculinity and to women's sense of femininity. Military officials argue over uniforms, especially where to put the pockets. There are government memos about where to place military women's pockets: they have to be functional and militarized, yet feminine. That can be a tricky formula to fulfill (Enloe 2000).

"I have applied for the SDF because the women entering the SDF can live on the base," begins a third woman who is imagining herself as an SDF woman volunteer. "If I don't have to pay for housing, I can save money. My plan is to stay inside the SDF for three or four years. Then, with the money I save, I will do postgraduate studies in Tokyo, get a professional certificate, and have an independent civilian career. So I see joining the SDF now merely as a means to an end. I'm not joining the SDF just to look for a husband, as I hear some other young women do. And I'm not interested in being a soldier. Honestly, I'm even a bit worried about the fact that the government is now sending warships and peacekeeping units overseas to the Middle East. Doesn't that violate Article 9? Well, I don't know much about politics. I just want to use the SDF as my own stepping-stone to an independent woman's life. I'll let the politicians worry about the big questions."

After hearing all these imagined women's voices, a woman toward the back stood up with determination. "I'm going to be myself. I'm for Article 9. I know what it means. That's one of the reasons I decided to join Tokyo's Women in Black. Well, 'join' isn't exactly what you do with Women in Black. It's a very loose and nonhierarchical group. We don't hold meetings or elect officers or pay dues or give speeches. Maybe you've heard of the Belgrade and the Jerusalem Women in Black groups. They've been nominated for the Nobel Peace Prize for the antiwar work they do in their countries. Here in Tokyo, any woman can just come and join our Friday evening vigils in Shinjuku. You can't miss us; we're the little circle of women with shoppers swirling around us. Some of the Friday night shoppers do pause to read our signs, and if they ask us questions, we do answer. Most of us try to come wearing something black. Any woman is welcome to join the circle. I see here in the audience tonight several women who come regularly. We stand silently at the bottom of the long outdoor subway escalator, in the glow of those huge neon signs. We keep our messages simple. We just hold up homemade signs saying 'Women against Violence' or 'No to War.' Last Friday some women wanted to make the links between peace and antiracism, so they brought along their own small signs that said 'Support the rights of Koreans in Japan.' After our hour's vigil, we usually go to a nearby Italian restaurant to have a bite of supper and get to know each other. Yes, Japanese peace activism, feminism, and Italian pasta can all go together!"

Few of the women and men who stood up that evening to take on the roles of women who had become militarized spoke explicitly of globalization. Yet each spoke from their own globalized consciousness. That is, each of these Japanese audience members who shared their ideas implied that even a woman living what seemed to be quite an apolitical and parochial life was thinking and acting within a web of international relationships.

Each participant there in the Tokyo auditorium also revealed how a militarizing process relies on the manipulation of diverse women's sense of their own femininity. In other words, militarization in any society (both in wartime and in alleged "peacetime") can be pushed forward only if diverse women's own beliefs about what it means to be "feminine" can be manipulated or exploited. Moreover, militarization—in Japan, but also in the United States, Britain, China, France, Russia, Israel, Syria, Turkey, Argentina, Colombia, Sudan—requires that the ideas about women's "femininity" held by women's and girls' families, employers, teachers, boyfriends, husbands, and political leaders be made to fit militarizing forms. As always, the politics of femininity is a tree with many branches and meandering subterranean roots.

What I have learned from my Japanese friends and colleagues is that we will be able to fully and accurately explain how and why militarization happens—or why sometimes it is stalled and occasionally is reversed—only when we sharpen our feminist curiosity, when we investigate the pressures shaping women's lives as well as women's own ideas about their work, their identities, their worries, and their desires.

Yet this sort of investigation is still often dismissed as not "real" politics. So changing what counts as "real" politics is a necessary part of getting a more subtly realistic—and reliable—grip on the causes and consequences of local and global militarization.

CHAPTER 9

CONCLUSION:
THE GLOBAL, THE LOCAL,
AND THE PERSONAL

The year 2014 was a good one for global arms sellers. According to the highly respected independent weapons monitoring group, the Stockholm International Peace Research Institute (SIPRI), during 2014 the world's total military expenditures reached a stunning $1.8 trillion (www.sipri.org). Of course, not every government was spending equal amounts of their citizens' tax contributions on purchasing arms for their militaries. In fact, Costa Rica and Iceland did not even have militaries. Of the world's total military expenditures, the United States accounted for a remarkable 34 percent. Moving down the scale, China that year ranked second, accounting for 12 percent of the world's total military expenditures. Saudi Arabia was third, with 5.4 percent of the total, Russia was fourth with 4.3 percent, and France was fifth with 3.5 percent.

Comparing SIPRI's totals for 2013 and 2014 military expenditures among geographic regions, North Africa, Sub-Saharan Africa, the Middle East, and Eastern Europe showed the largest increases in their governments' military expenditures; at the same time, North America and Western and Central Europe showed the most notable drops in expenditures. Militarized crises in Syria and Iraq, together with those of Eastern Ukraine and the Great Lakes of Africa, however, already were pushing some governments to increase their military budget proposals for the upcoming years.

In late 2015, a terrorist attack on a Russian civilian plane carrying Russian vacationers home from Egyptian seaside resorts and, shortly thereafter, terrorist attacks that killed dozens of civilians in Beirut and Paris, together convinced many officials that the only viable response to such attacks was a militarized response: raiding neighborhoods, tightening borders, rejecting refugees, increasing the powers of surveillance agencies, expanding military operations at home and abroad, and discounting violations of civil liberties and wartime "collateral damage" as the inevitable price to be paid for promised security. Many ordinary citizens agreed.

Jet fighters, armored vehicles, missiles, computer software, and heavy artillery are not cheap. A lot of governments are spending large slices of their limited resource pies to act out their militarized visions of "national security." The high percentages of public funds being spent on militarized security do raise the eyebrows of many American, Saudi, Ugandan, Sudanese, Russian, Iranian, British, French, Mexican, Japanese, Korean, and Chinese citizens. Though some of these skeptical citizens are afraid to voice their concerns out loud, these civilians wonder whether the same public funds might be better spent on other projects that would enhance their fellow citizens' security—by improving schools, expanding and upgrading medical care, developing new environmental protections, challenging practices of racist and sexist discrimination, stepping up workplace safety inspections, offering training programs for the unemployed and the underemployed, and supporting newly arrived refugees.

A lot of governments' military spending is for arms bought and sold internationally. The weaponry market has indeed become globalized. That is, it is not just Nike, Sony, BMW, Disney, and Dunlop that are globally marketing their products and encouraging potential consumers to develop needs and desires they may not have thought they had. So too are manufacturers of heavy and light weapons. Most of these weapons manufacturers' customers are governments. Usually, government officials from each weapons manufacturer's home country see themselves as commercial enablers: they perceive their own public responsibility as one of helping their country's manufacturers win sales of their militarized products abroad. Playing this role—and perceiving this as among their public duties—serves to militarize the mindsets of many civilian officials working in departments of trade, commerce, and industry.

Returning to SIPRI's careful annual reports, the world's list of top 100 arms sellers is dominated by companies based in North America and Western Europe. Together, those companies account for 84 percent of the global arms sales. Russia-based companies' sales have been growing, but their sales pale next to those of their U.S. and Western European global competitors. Other governments have been promoting their own arms makers. Among today's so-called "emerging producers" (and sellers) of arms are companies based in Brazil, India, South Korea, Singapore, and Turkey. Because of China's lack of transparency, its weapons manufacturers (most of them state-owned companies) have been very difficult even for SIPRI's researchers to track.

Nonetheless, the world's top five companies producing and selling military equipment and military services (for instance, training) are overwhelmingly American: Lockheed Martin (USA), Boeing (USA), BAE Systems (UK), Raytheon (USA), and Northrop Grumman (USA) (Fleurant and Perlo-Freeman 2014). To make sense of each of these companies, one has to investigate them not just as profit-seeking, but also as patriarchal (www.reachingcriticalwill.org).

As we have seen, militarization can be woven into the lives of many more people than just those in uniform or those who work in defense ministries or national security agencies. Civilian mental health workers can become militarized, for instance, if, when working with military veterans, they begin to see their professional goal as addressing only those veterans' mental health needs while deliberately steering clear of the risky territory of those soldiers' moral responsibility. The width and depth of that professional silence becomes a measure of both the therapists' and their profession's militarization (Scandlyn and Hautzinger 2015). The enforcers of militarized silence are diverse. For instance, media commentators, bloggers, film critics, moviegoers, and family members each nurture patriarchal militarized silences when they try to block out women's candid tellings of their complex experiences of surviving wartime rape, tellings that could challenge facile post-war narratives of national unity (Chowdhury 2015).

Similarly, civilian engineers or physicists pursuing a corporate career in an arms manufacturing firm can become militarized insofar as they decide not to question the uses to which their knowledge and skills are being put. So too can their spouses, if they see their partners' militarized work as important for their own sense of economic security or social status. The mayors of towns where an arms maker has its manufacturing plant will be militarized insofar as those mayors, concerned about local jobs and local tax revenues, cheer every time that the arms company wins a new government contract or makes a big overseas sale. Civilian treasury or finance officials can become militarized to the extent that they worry about the gap between their country's imports and exports, and thus are relieved to see overseas arms exports sales narrowing that imbalance of payments. Militarization also can infiltrate the life of a mid-level commerce or industry official whose performance will be judged on the basis of whether she or he succeeds in "opening overseas markets" for local arms manufacturers.

The sorts of companies now competing for defense contracts are more diverse than ever. A generation ago it was chiefly the makers of arms and high-tech weapons that were throwing their corporate hats into the defense-contracting ring. Nowadays to track commercial militarization, we need to cast our curiosity much more widely. Today, construction companies; software developers; advertising companies; the providers of food services, health services, banking services, telephone services, and entertainment services, as well as private intelligence consultants are joining the weapons makers in bidding for military contracts.

The person who offered this caveat is a former director of SIPRI. At a seminar held in Stockholm, Alyson Bailes, herself a career British diplomat before becoming the head of SIPRI, warned other attendees not to complacently imagine that women are positioned in the economy so that they are less likely to be militarized. That is, just because the majority of assembly workers and technical employees of arms manufacturers are men does not mean women are immune from the appeals of militarized work. Alyson Bailes warned her listeners that not only are women breaking into these formerly masculinized defense industry fields, but, in addition, a lot more women today are making their way up corporate executive ladders of diverse sorts of companies—for instance, specializing in services and media—and thus will likely face decisions about whether it is good—or risky—for their own companies to join the competition to win government defense contracts.

Among the newest military "products" being bought and sold globally are soldiers themselves. Mercenaries are not new. There were mercenaries fighting in the American Revolution of the late eighteenth century. What is new is the scope of the sale and purchase of soldiers to travel the world to fight the wars of other governments. "Private military companies" and "private security companies" are now categories of private firms selling personnel's service globally. By the middle of the U.S.-led Iraq War, for instance, there were more militarized privately contracted personnel in Iraq than there were U.S. government military personnel. Most private military and security firms are American and British. But today, as more governments are in the market for privatized soldiers, other entrepreneurs are joining the international competition (Higate 2012a). One of the distinguishing features of this globalized trade in privatized military and security personnel is its masculinization. That is, the personnel whose services these companies sell to governments are both overwhelmingly male *and* their salable characteristic is their masculinized approach to soldiering (Eichler 2015; Higate 2012b).

Among the governments that now are hiring foreign private military companies are those of Saudi Arabia and the United Arab Emirates. The Saudi government has hired Sudanese men to help them wage their ground war in Yemen, while Saudi men pilot the jet fighters waging war from the air over Yemen. The UAE has hired a Colombian private military company, Global Enterprises, to recruit hundreds of Colombian men recently retired from the Colombian government's military. Global Enterprises was launched by an entrepreneurial Colombian army veteran who had commanded his government's special operations forces, among the most masculinized branches of Colombia's military. The new male recruits hired by Global Enterprises were attracted by the relatively high salaries paid to them by the government of UAE. While their Colombian military pay was $400 per month, their new employers would pay them $2,000–3,000 per month, with a bonus of $1,000 per week if they are deployed to fight with the Saudi-UAE wartime coalition in Yemen. Once in their UAE desert training camps, these now-privatized Colombian male soldiers reportedly sent most of their money home to their Colombian families (Hager and Mazzetti 2015).

In other words, these private masculinized soldiers were fighting in part as husbands and fathers. The wives of men hired by the growing number of globalized private military and security companies thereby become integral to these companies' global operations. These women's gendered marriages become both globalized and militarized.

As government defense officials multiply the products and services that they privatize—that is, that they farm out to private, civilian companies—more and more women with MBAs seeking to use their skills and talents in the world of private business will be prone to militarization. No longer will women executives be somewhat less subject to direct militarization simply because they are not working for companies that produce rifles, night-vision goggles, body armor, missiles, and submarines. These women executives—trying to gain markets for their food products, telephone services, magazines, computer games, housing services—also will be more likely to have to decide whether their firms should depend for any part of their profits on helping any military achieve its goals.

This serves as a warning: militarization has to be tracked over a long time. A short attention span can lead the tracker to flawed explanations. Flawed explanations generate flawed prescriptions.

The changes in defense contracting suggest another caveat: to track militarization one needs to monitor changing gender patterns within diverse organizations, as well as the pressures on those trying to graduate from outsider to insider status within those competitive worlds.

As we have seen, militarization is a process that binds together the personal, the local, the national, and the global. For instance, one can look at college students today in Massachusetts who have chosen to major in engineering. How will they—and their parents and professors—react to the following newspaper article? "Prodded by state government officials fearful of alienating a key Massachusetts industry, nine Bay State colleges and universities have agreed to adapt their engineering curriculums, and in some cases introduce new courses, to meet the needs of defense contractors" (Weisman 2006).

The reporter goes on to describe how the Massachusetts state governor and his economic development aides are worried that if Massachusetts colleges do not train students in the sorts of skills desired by locally based, globally competing defense contractors—for example,

Raytheon and Lockheed Martin—those companies might lose future U.S. and overseas defense bids, which in turn, would damage the state's entire economy. This calculation suggests that already the state's economy has become significantly militarized; that is, it has become dependent not only on companies whose profits come from defense work, but on the principal source of defense monies, the military.

How did the presidents, deans, and faculty of Massachusetts' colleges respond to the industry's call? Worcester Polytechnic Institute (WPI), the University of Massachusetts, Wentworth Institute of Technology, Northeastern University, Boston University, and Cape Cod Community College accepted defense-contracting companies' invitation to discuss the companies' curricular needs, such as new courses in defense-contract management and radio frequency engineering (Weisman 2006). If a young man or woman at WPI or Northeastern today decides to follow an advisor's suggestion and take a course in radio frequency engineering, will he or she understand the militarizing process he or she is joining? Perhaps the young man or woman will be aware. Perhaps militarization will look to the student like the path to a well-paying and secure career, as well as a way to contribute to his or her country's national security and a healthy balance of import and export payments.

So militarization can appear attractive. It can be personally rewarding, both materially and emotionally. It can seem to make sense and be practical and efficient. Militarization can seem to be a reasonable response to a threat-filled, unpredictable world. In fact, the more convinced any person becomes of globalized or localized danger, the more likely he or she is to see the prioritization of military needs and militaristic values over other needs and values as positive, or at least inevitable.

Ideas matter. The idea that the world is a dangerous place is the seed of many militarizing processes. Alternative ideas portray the world as full of human creativity, the potential for human cooperation, or opportunities for empathy and mutual respect. Many efforts taking place now—in Turkey, Afghanistan, Syria, Canada, Colombia, Bosnia, Iceland, Egypt, Tunisia, Norway, Nepal, the United States, Sweden, Israel, Congo, Iran, India, Liberia, Haiti, Indonesia, Britain, South Korea, Serbia, Japan—to demilitarize societies are attempts to alter deep-seated, widely held ideas:

- ideas about pride
- ideas about threats
- ideas about protectors
- ideas about citizenship
- ideas about race
- ideas about modernity
- ideas about bravery
- ideas about history
- ideas about rationality
- ideas about security
- ideas about violence
- ideas about trust

Each of these ideas is fraught with blatant and subtle presumptions about masculinity and femininity. Ideas about both masculinity and femininity matter. These gendered ideas gain potency when they are laced with ideas about "the other"—ideas about race, ethnicity, class, and religion. This complex reality turns gender analysis skills and feminist curiosity into necessities for the careful tracker of militarization—whether global, local, or personal. Equipped with a gender analytical tool kit and a lively feminist curiosity, the tracker is most likely to always ask about the politics of masculinities and of femininities: Who benefits from which notions about masculinity? Who has the resources to make their presumptions about femininity the basis for foreign policy? And how do particular men and women making their homes in places as different as Miami, Tokyo, Moscow, and Damascus live with the consequences of those gender-fueled policies?

For example, as we have seen, ideas about "security" can be interpreted so that they assign priority to the government's military, which in turn tends to put the mostly male national security elite in positions of exceptional authority. On the other hand, "security" could be interpreted to mean what it takes for women as well as men to feel safe inside their own homes and neighborhoods or in refugee camps. This alternative interpretation of "security" would accord less authority to military experts and more authority to local women's groups whose activists have been collecting information about women's daily lives and devising ways to prevent rape and domestic violence.

Similarly, one needs to keep a sharp feminist eye on ideas about "protectors." Are the most effective protectors thought to be those trained to wield weaponry? If so, then again this interpretation is likely to make soldiers—and those with the authority to deploy them—seem to be the most dependable protectors. Since in most countries today 85–100 percent of all soldiers are male, women are cast as the protected. Protectors, in turn, are imagined to be the "action figures" in civic life—those who not only can move around (they are not tied down by domestic responsibilities) but can, it is frequently imagined, think rationally about which moves are most needed now and which moves can be shoved down the priority agenda until "later." Once more, the gendered interpretation of any one of these ideas will have implications for gendered thinking about other ideas on this list.

Ideas, however, don't just float out there on the breeze. Ideas gain legitimacy and influence—or are quashed and discredited—within particular social settings: classrooms, television studios and newsrooms, legislatures, beauty parlors, interrogation cells, closed-doors strategy sessions, business meetings, courtrooms, cafes, and banter-filled locker rooms. All of these turn into sites for listening: listening for the making and unmaking of those ideas about masculinity and about femininity that will move militarization forward—or roll it back.

Institutions and organizations are riddled with presumptions about and practices of femininity and masculinity. For example, within a given organization, one can be on the lookout for what sort of person is deemed rational enough to make the "Big Decisions." One can pay close attention to what sorts of labor are dismissed as "unskilled" and are thus low paid. One can note what sorts of people are thought by others to be "experts," who is written off as "emotional." The answers to these questions will determine whose ideas about "security" will hold sway as the organization goes about its day-to-day business.

No idea gains primacy or is imagined "normal" at the snap of the fingers. It takes time and many steps—most of them hardly visible, many of them seemingly trivial—for instance, for "national security" to become militarized, for soldiers to become civilians' chief protectors, for a woman to become a "military wife," for an abuser to become merely a lone "bad apple," or for men to become ashamed of any suggestion that they are "feminine."

As a result, tracking militarization—the interplay of ideas and social relationships over time—calls upon the tracker to "think big" and "think small" simultaneously. The astute tracker of militarization will listen for the jokes, read the daily memos, chart what is not said. At the same time, the tracker of militarization will put the pieces together in order to gradually map the larger patterns—the landscape, the doctrine, the culture, the organizational climate, the system. Jokes and the culture; memos and the system; silences and the climate; apples, the barrel, and the orchard.

When gendered militarization becomes globalized, it works its way through ideas on the wings of institutions and organizations. This means that in order for us to track the many paths by which militarization travels, we need to stay deeply interested in the personal, the local, and the national, while we also widen our lens to watch how those militarizing ideas, organizations, and processes move across territorial borders.

The gender-smart tracker of globalizing militarization will thus develop a feminist curiosity about the workings of alliances, humanitarian organizations, international agencies, international media, and international trade; and the international movement of people as immigrants, soldiers, insurgents, refugees, and diplomats.

Yes, it is a tall order. And today the analytical order is getting taller and taller. Being realistic about today's globalizing militarization—how and why it happens, what its consequences are—is not a modest goal.

Those who have come to the conclusion that demilitarization is an honorable and valuable objective will need to develop the same tracking skills. The gender-smart pursuer of demilitarization will need to make sense of how militarization occurs in the lives of individuals and families, in companies, in institutions, in nations, and across national borders.

There are steps being taken toward demilitarization—by students who ask that the history of peace movements be taught in ordinary history or political science courses, by parents who rethink what it means for a son to "become a man," by computer companies that decide to eschew defense contracts, by women's groups that pressure foreign aid managers to redefine "security," by activists and diplomats who help create new treaties and institutions to outlaw land mines, torture, child soldiers, ethnic cleansing, and wartime rape. Some of these steps will prove only temporary, soon to be stymied or reversed. Which steps will produce lasting transformations?

Tracking militarization and fostering demilitarization call for cooperative investigations, multiple skills, and the appreciation of diverse perspectives. Simultaneous gender-aware attention to the personal, the local, the national, and the global cannot be done alone.

REFERENCES

AeroWeb. 2014. "Top 100 Defense Contractors 2014." http://www.bga-aeroweb .com.

Aharoni, Sarai, and Rula Deeb. 2005. *Where Are All the Women? UN Security Council Resolution 1325: Gender Perspectives of the Israeli-Palestinian Conflict*. Haifa, Israel: Isha L'Isha–Haifa Feminist Center and Kayan Feminist Organization.

Al-Ali, Nadje, and Nicola Pratt. 2009. *What Kind of Liberation? Women and the Occupation of Iraq*. Berkeley: University of California Press.

Alexievich, Svetlana. 1992. *Zinky Boys: Soviet Voices from the Afghan War*. New York: W.W. Norton and Co.

Altinay, Ayse Gul. 2004. *The Myth of the Military Nation: Militarism, Gender, and Education in Turkey*. New York: Palgrave Macmillan.

Altinay, Ayse Gul and Andrea Peto, eds. 2016. *Gendered Wars, Gendered Memories*. Farnham, UK: Ashgate.

Alva, Donna. 2006. *Unofficial Ambassadors: American Military Families and the Cold War, 1945–1965*. New York: New York University Press.

Alvarez, Lizette. 2006. "Military Fails Some Widows Over Benefits." *New York Times*, June 27.

Amnesty International, International Action Network on Small Arms, and Oxfam International. 2006. *The Impact of Guns on Women's Lives*. Control Arms. http://www.controlarms.org.documents/small-arms-women-report-final2-1.pdf.

Arditti, Rita. 1999. *Searching for Life: The Grandmothers of the Plaza de Mayo and the Disappeared Children of Argentina*. Berkeley: University of California Press.

Associated Press. 2006. "Dog Handler Convicted in Abu Ghraib Abuse." *New York Times*, June 2.

Ballinger, Jeff. 2010. "The Threat Posed by 'Corporate Social Responsibility' to Trade Union Rights." In *Fair Trade, Corporate Accountability*, ed. Surrey Farnham, 223–240. London: Ashgate.

Barkawi, Tarak. 2006. *Globalization and War*. Lanham, MD: Rowman & Littlefield.

Basch, Linda. 2005. "Human Security, Globalization, and Feminist Visions." *Peace Review* 16 (1): 5–12.

Basham, Victoria, 2013. *War, Identity and the Liberal State*. London and New York: Routledge, 2013.

Basham, Victoria, Aaron Belkin, and Jess Gifkins. 2015. "Editorial," *Critical Military Studies* 1(1): 1–2.

Baydar, Gülsüm, and Berfin Ivegen. 2006. "Territories, Identities, and Thresholds: The Saturday Mothers Phenomenon in Istanbul." *Signs* 31(3): 689–716.

Bauer, Jan, and Anissa Helie. 2006. *Documenting Women's Rights Violations by Non-State Actors: Activist Strategies for Muslim Countries*. Montreal: Rights and Democracy.

Beier, Marshall. 2004. 'Emailed Applications Are Preferred': Ethical Practices in Mine Action and the Idea of Global Civil Society." In *The Future of Humanitarian Mine Action*, ed. Kristian Berg Harpviken, 19–32. New York: Palgrave Macmillan.

Bolkovac, Katherine, with Cari Lynn. 2011. *The Whistleblower*. New York: Palgrave Macmillan.

Bowers, Simon. 2004. "Merrill Lynch Accused of 'Institutional Sexism.'" *Guardian* (London), June 12.

Broder, John M., David S. Cloud, John Kifner, Carolyn Marshall, Eric Schmitt, and Thom Shanker. 2006. "Contradictions Cloud Inquiry into 24 Iraqi Deaths." *New York Times*, June 17.

Brown, Kate. 2013. *Plutopia*. London and New York: Oxford University Press.

Brownfield-Stein, Chava. 2006. "An Army That Has a State? The Role of Israel's Security Establishment in a Comparative Perspective," Paper presented at the Van Leer Institute, Jerusalem, Israel, June 5.

Buchanan, Rose Troup, 2015, "4 in 10 Women in the Military Are Victims of Sexual Harassment, New Survey Finds," London: *The Independent*, July 14.

Bunster-Burotto, Ximena. 1985. "Surviving Beyond Fear: Women and Torture in Latin America." In *Women and Change in Latin America*, ed. June Nash and Helen Safa, 297–325. South Hadley, MA: Bergin & Garvey.

Burke, Carol. 2004. *Camp All-American, Hanoi Jane, and the High-and-Tight*. Boston: Beacon Press.

———. 2006. "One of the Boys." *Women's Review of Books* 23 (2): 3–5.

Burns, John F. 2006. "Getting Used to War as Hell." *New York Times*, June 4.

Butalia, Urvashi, ed. 2012. *Women's Voices from Kashmir*. Delhi: Kali for Women.

Callimachi, Rukmin. 2015. "ISIS and the Lonely Young American." *New York Times*, June 28.

Caraway, Teri L. 2007. *Assembling Women: The Feminization of Global Manufacturing*. Ithaca: Cornell University Press.

Carver, Terrell. 2003. "Gender/Feminism/IR." *International Studies Review* 5 (2): 288–290.

Chan-Tiberghien, Jennifer. 2004. *Gender and Human Rights in Japan*. Stanford, CA: Stanford University Press.

Chang, Patty et al. 2015. *Women Leading Peace*, Washington, DC: Georgetown Institute for Women, Peace and Security.

Chesto, Jon. 2015. "Military Foot Race." *Boston Globe*, June 6.

Chike. 2014. "Riots in Vietnam Sneaker Factories." Sneaker Watch. May 22. http://www.sneakerwatch.com.

Chisholm, Amanda. 2014. "The Silenced and Indispensible: Gurkhas in Private Security Companies." *International Feminist Journal of Politics*. 16 (1): 26–47.

Chowdhury, Elora Halim. 2015. "When Love and Violence Meet: Women's Agency and Transformative Politics in Rubaiyat Hossain's 'Meherjaan.'" *Hypatia* 30 (4): 760–777.

Cinar, Ozgur Heval and Coskun Usterci, eds. 2009. *Conscientious Objection*. London and New York: Zed Books.

Cloud, David S. 2006. "Inquiry Suggests Marines Excised Files on Killings." *New York Times*, August 18.

Cock, Jacklyn. 1995. "Forging a New Army out of Old Enemies: Women in the South African Military." In "Rethinking Women's Peace Studies," special issue, *Women's Studies Quarterly* 23 (3–4): 97–111.

Cockburn, Cynthia. 2007. *From Where We Stand: War, Women's Activism, and Feminist Analysis*. London: Zed Books.

———. 2012. *Anti-Militarism*. London and New York: Palgrave Macmillan.

Cockburn, Cynthia, and Dubravka Zarkov, eds. 2002. *The Postwar Moment: Militaries, Masculinities, and International Peacekeeping*. London: Lawrence & Wishart.

Coghan, Tom. 2006. "Afghan MP Says She Will Not Be Silenced." Reprinted in *Women Living Under Muslim Law Newsletter* 18 (April): 4.

Cohn, Carol. 1987. "Sex and Death in the Rational World of Defense Intellectuals." *Signs* 12 (4): 687–718.

———, ed. 2013. *Women and Wars*. Cambridge: Polity Press.

Cohn, Carol, with Felicity Hill and Sara Ruddick. 2005. *The Relevance of Gender for Eliminating Weapons of Mass Destruction*. Stockholm: Institute for Disarmament Diplomacy.

Coleman, Isobel, and Swanee Hunt. 2006. "Afghanistan Should Make Room for Its Female Leaders." *Christian Science Monitor*, April 24.

Confortini, Catia. 2012. *Intelligent Compassion: Critical Feminist Methodology in the Women's League for Peace and Freedom*. London and New York: Oxford University Press.

Conway, Daniel. 2012. *Masculinities, Militarisation and the End Conscription Campaign: War Resistance in Apartheid South Africa*. Manchester and New York: Manchester University Press.

Danner, Mark, ed. 2004. *Torture and Truth: America, Abu Ghraib, and the War on Terror*. New York: New York Review of Books.

Domosh, Mona. 2006. *American Commodities in an Age of Empire*. New York: Routledge.

Eager, Paige Whaley. 2004. *Global Population Policy: From Population Control to Reproductive Rights*. London: Ashgate.

———. 2014. *Waging Gendered Wars*. London: Ashgate.

Editorial Board. 2015. "Will Anyone Pay for Abu Ghraib?" *New York Times*, February 5.

NBC News. 2013. "Iraq War 10 Years Later: Where Are They Now? Lynndie England." March 19.

Ehrenreich, Barbara. 2004. "All Together Now." Op-Ed, *New York Times*, July 15.

Eichler, Maya. 2012. *Militarizing Men: Gender, Conscription and War in Post-Soviet Russia*, Stanford: Stanford University Press.

———, ed. 2015. *Gender and Private Security in Global Politics*. London and New York: Oxford University Press.

Elias, Juanita, ed. 2009. "Hegemonic Masculinities in International Politics." Special issue, *Men and Masculinities* 10 (4).

Enloe, Cynthia. 1980. *Ethnic Soldiers: State Security in Divided Societies*. London: Penguin.

———. 1993. *The Morning After: Sexual Politics at the End of the Cold War*. Berkeley: University of California Press.

———. 2000. *Maneuvers: The International Politics of Militarizing Women's Lives*. Berkeley: University of California Press.

———. 2004. *The Curious Feminist: Searching for Women in a New Age of Empire*. Berkeley: University of California Press.

———. 2010. *Nimo's War, Emma's War: Making Feminist Sense of the Iraq War*. Berkeley: University of California Press.

———. 2013. *Seriously! Investigating Crashes and Crises As If Women Mattered*. Berkeley: University of California Press.

———. 2014. *Bananas, Beaches and Bases: Making Feminist Sense of International Politics*. Berkeley: University of California Press. updated 2nd edition.

———. 2015. "The Recruiter and the Skeptic: A Critical Approach to Military Studies." *Critical Military Studies* (1) 1: 3–10.

Eran-Jona, Meytal. 2005. "The Sailor's Girl: Gender Regime and the Militarization of Military Wives in the IDF." Research paper, Department of Sociology, Tel Aviv University.

Farr, Vanessa. 2006. "Gender Analysis as a Tool for Multilateral Negotiators in the Small Arms Context." In *Disarmament as Humanitarian Action*, ed. John Borrie and Vanessa Martin Randin, 109–136. Geneva: United Nations Institute for Disarmament Research.

Farr, Vanessa, and Kiflemiriam Gebre-Wold, eds. 2002. *Gender Perspectives on Small Arms and Light Weapons*. Brief 24. Bonn, Germany: Bonn International Center for Conversion, July.

Fellowship of Reconciliation. 2005. "Petition to Support Article 9 of the Japanese Constitution." Amsterdam: Fellowship of Reconciliation.

Ferguson, Kathy, and Monique Mironesco, eds. 2008. *Gender and Globalization in Asia and the Pacific*. Honolulu: University of Hawaii Press.

Fleurant, Aude and Sam Perlo-Freeman. 2014. "The SIPRI Top 100 Arms-Producing and Military Services Companies, 2013." Stockholm: Stockholm International Peace Research Institute.

Fox, Mary-Jane. 2004. "Girl Soldiers." *Security Dialogue* 35 (4): 465–480.

Frühstück, Sabine. 2006. *Uneasy Warriors: Gender, Memory, and Popular Culture in the Japanese Army*. Berkeley: University of California Press.

Giles, Wenona, Malathi de Alwis, Edith Klein, and Neluka Silva, eds. 2003. *Feminists Under Fire: Exchanges Across War Zones*. Toronto: Between the Lines.

Gillan, Audrey. 2005. "The Great Gurkha Race." *Guardian* (London), June 12.

Gillem, Mark. 2007. *America Town: Building the Outposts of Empire*. Minneapolis: University of Minnesota Press.

Golden, Tim. 2006. "The Battle for Guantanamo." *New York Times Magazine*, September 17, 60–71, 140–145.

Goldenberg, Suzanne. 2006. "Woman Soldier Refuses Return to Iraq, Claiming Sexual Harassment." *Guardian* (London), June 21.

Greenberg, Karen, and Joshua Dratel, eds. 2005. *The Torture Papers: The Road to Abu Ghraib*. New York: Cambridge University Press.

Greenhouse, Linda. 2006. "Supreme Court Blocks Guantanamo Tribunals." *New York Times*, July 6.

Gusterson, Hugh. 1996. *Nuclear Rites: A Weapons Laboratory at the End of the Cold War*. Berkeley: University of California Press.

Hager, Emily B. and Mark Mazzetti. 2015. "Emirates Secretly Sends Colombian Mercenaries to Yemen Fight." *New York Times*, November 26.

Halili, Idan. 2006. "Interview with Feminist Refusnik Idan Halili," Tel Aviv, Quaker Service.

Hansen, Lene, and Louise Olsson, eds. 2004. "Gender and Security." Special issue, *Security Dialogue* 35 (4).

Harrison, Deborah. 2002. *The First Casualty: Violence Against Women in Canadian Military Communities*. Toronto: James Lorimer & Co.

Harrison, Deborah, and Lucie Laliberte. 1994. *No Life Like It: Military Wives in Canada*. Toronto: James Lorimer & Co.

Hartmann, Betsy. 1995. *Reproductive Rights and Wrongs: The Global Politics of Population Control and Contraceptive Choice*, rev. ed. Boston: South End Press.

Hawkesworth, Mary. 2006. *Globalization and Feminist Activism*. Lanham, MD: Rowman & Littlefield.

Henry, Monica K. 2006. "'Good Military Wives' Stay 'In the Closet': Obstacles to Openly Opposing Operation Iraq Freedom (OIF)." Unpublished master's thesis, San Jose, Costa Rica, Gender and Peacebuilding Program, UN University for Peace.

Henson, Maria Rose. 1999. *Comfort Woman: A Filipina's Story*. Boulder, CO: Rowman and Littlefield.

Hersh, Seymour M. 2004. *Chain of Command: The Road to Abu Ghraib*. New York: HarperCollins.

Higate, Paul. 2012a. "The Private Militarized and Security Contractor as Geocorporeal Actor." Bristol: School of Sociology, Politics and International Studies, University of Bristol. Working Paper No. 09–12.

———. 2012b. "Cowboys and Professionals: The Politics of Identity Work in the Private and Military Security Company." *Millennium Journal of International Studies* 40 (2): 321–341.

Higate, Paul, and Marsha Henry. 2004. "Gender in Peace Support Operations." In "Gender and Security," ed. Lene Hansen and Louise Olsson, special issue, *Security Dialogue* 35 (4): 481–498.

Hill, Felicity, Mikele Aboitiz, and Sara Poehlman-Doumbouya. 2003. "Nongovernmental Organizations' Roles in the Buildup and Implementation of Security Council Resolution 1325." *Signs* 28 (4): 1255–1270.

Hill, Felicity, Carol Cohn, and Cynthia Enloe. 2006. "U.N. Security Council Resolution 1325 Three Years On: Gender, Security, and Organizational Change." Boston: Boston Consortium on Gender, Security, and Human Rights.

Hillman, Elizabeth Lutes. 2005. *Defending America: Military Culture and the Cold War Court-Martial*. Princeton: Princeton University Press.

Hindustan Times. 2006. "Women on Top in Peace Force." June 6.

Hirshberg, Lauren. 2012. "Nuclear Families: (Re)Producing 1950s Suburban America in the Marshall Islands," *OAH Magazine of History*. 26 (4).

Holmquist, Caroline. 2005. *Private Security Companies: The Case for Regulation*. Stockholm: Stockholm International Peace Research Institute.

Hoogensen, Gunhild, and Kirsti Stuvoy. 2006. "Gender Resistance and Human Security." *Security Dialogue* 37 (2): 207–228.

Hooper, Charlotte. 2001. *Manly States: Masculinities, International Relations, and Gender Politics*. New York: Columbia University Press.

Houppert, Karen. 2005. *Home Fires Burning: Married to the Military—For Better or for Worse*. New York: Ballantine.

Human Rights Watch. 2004. *The Road to Abu Ghraib*. New York: Human Rights Watch.

Humanas Corporacion Colombia. 2013. *La Violencia Sexual Una Estrategia para Militar en Colombia*. Bogota: Humanas Corporacion Colombia.

Hyde, Alexandra, 2015. "Inhabiting No-Man's Land: The Military Mobilities of Army Wives." PhD Dissertation. London School of Economics and Politics.

Ito, Ruri. 2006. "The Modern Girl Question in 1920s and '30s Okinawa: Colonial Modernity and Women's Mobility." *Journal of Gender Studies* 9: 1–18.

Ito, Ruri, and Yasuyo Morimoto. 2004. "The Modern Girl and Colonial Modernity in East Asia: An International Collaborative Project." *Journal of Gender Studies* 7: 111–114.

Jacobson, Agneta Soderberg. 2005. *Security on Whose Terms: If Men and Women Were Equal*. Stockholm: Kvinna Till Kvinna: Women's Empowerment Projects.

Jaffer, Nabeelah. 2015. "The Sisters of ISIS," London: *The Guardian*, June 25.

Jargon, Julie. 2003. "The War Within." *Westword*, January 30. http://www.westword.com/issues/2003-01-30/feature.html.

Jehl, Douglas. 2004. "Some Abu Ghraib Abuses Are Traced to Afghanistan." *New York Times*, August 26.

Johnson, Chalmers. 2003. *Sorrows of Empire: Militarism, Secrecy, and the End of the Republic*. New York: Metropolitan Books.

Joshi, Vijaya. 2005. "Building Opportunities: Women's Organizing, Militarism, and the United Nations Transitional Administration in East Timor." PhD diss., Clark University.

Jowers, Karen. 2014. "Some Fast Food Outlets Closing on Military Bases." *Army Times*. March 17.

Kang, Stephanie. 2006. "The Swoosh Treads Lightly at Chic Converse." *Globe and Mail* (Toronto), June 23.

Karpinski, Janis. 2005. *One Woman's Army: The Commanding General of Abu Ghraib Tells Her Story*. New York: Hyperion.

———. 2007. "Lynndie England in Love." In *Women as Aggressors and Torturers*, ed. Tara McKelvey. Seattle: Seal Press.

Kashiwazaki, Tomoko. 2006. "VAWW Net Japan's Campaign to Bring Justice for the Survivors of Wartime Sexual Slavery." Asia Pacific Forum on Women, Law and Development, *Forum News* 19 (January-April): 22.

Katzenstein, Mary Fainsod. 1998. *Faithful and Fearless: Moving Feminist Protest Inside the Church and Military*. Princeton: Princeton University Press.

Kaufman, Joyce and Kristen Williams. 2010. *Women and War*. Sterling, VA: Kumarian Press.

Kim, Seung-Kyung. 1997. *Class Struggle or Family Struggle: The Lives of Women Factory Workers in South Korea*. London: Cambridge University Press.

Koonz, Claudia. 2003. *The Nazi Conscience*. Cambridge, MA: Harvard University Press.

Koppel, Ted. 2006. "These Guns for Hire." *New York Times*, May 22.

Krauss, Clifford. 2006. "Canada Leader Wins in Extending Afghan Tour." *New York Times*, May 18.

Kronsell, Annica. 2012. *Postnational Defense*. London and New York: Oxford University Press.

Krosch, Sara L. 2005. "'A New Race of Women': The Challenges of Reintegrating Eritrea's Demobilized Female Combatants." Research paper, Department of International Development, Community and Environment, Clark University.

Kwon, Insook. 1998. "'The New Women's Movement' in 1920s Korea: Rethinking the Relationship Between Imperialism and Women" in "Feminisms and Internationalism," special issue, *Gender and History* 10 (3): 381–405.

———. 2000. " Militarism in My Heart: Militarization of Women's Consciousness and Culture in South Korea." PhD diss., Clark University.

———. 2005. "How Identities and Movement Cultures Became Deeply Saturated with Militarism: Lessons from the Pro-democracy Movement in South Korea." *Asian Journal of Women's Studies* 11 (2): 7–40.

Lang, Amy and Cecilia Tachi, eds. 2006. *What Democracy Looks Like*. New Brunswick, NJ: Rutgers University Press.

Lardner, Richard and Eileen Sullivan. 2015. "Military Sex Case Justice Called Hazy," *Boston Globe*, November 19.

Laufer, Peter. 2006. *Mission Rejected: US Soldiers Who Say No to Iraq.* White River Junction, VT: Chelsea Green.

Lawson, Mark. 2006. "The Sex War's New Frontier: We Fight for Equality, Yet Balk at the Death of a Woman in Action in Iraq." London: *Guardian.* May 12.

Lewis, Neil A., and Eric Schmitt. 2004. "Lawyers Decided Bans on Torture Didn't Bind Bush." *New York Times,* June 8.

Lewis, Stephen. 2005. *Race Against Time.* Toronto: House of Anasi Press.

Lipman, Jana K. 2009. *Guantánamo: A Working Class History Between Empire and Revolution.* Berkeley: University of California Press.

Lipman, Jana K., and Daniel Bender, eds. 2015. *Making the Empire Work: Labor and United States Imperialism.* New York: New York University Press.

Lutz, Catherine. 2001. *Homefront: A Military City and the American Twentieth Century.* Boston: Beacon Press.

———, ed. 2009. *The Bases of Empire: The Global Struggle Against U.S. Military Posts.* London: Pluto Press.

Lutz, Catherine, and Jon Elliston. 2004. "Domestic Terror." In *Interventions: Activists' and Academics' Perspectives on Violence*, ed. Elizabeth Castelli and Janet Jackson. New York: Palgrave Macmillan.

Mackenzie, Megan. 2012. *Female Soldiers in Sierra Leone.* New York: NYU Press.

———. 2015. *Beyond the Band of Brothers.* Cambridge and New York: Cambridge University Press.

Maley, Jacqueline. 2006. "Sexual Harassment Rife in Armed Forces." *Guardian* (London), May 26.

Manning, Lory. 2005. *Women in the Military: Where They Stand.* 5th ed. Washington, DC: Women's Research and Education Institute.

———. 2006. *Proceedings of the Conference Women in the Military Today.* Washington, DC: Women's Research and Education Institute.

Marshall, Carolyn. 2006. "On a Marine Base, Disbelief over Charges." *New York Times,* May 30.

Mater, Nadire. 2005. *Voices from the Front: Turkish Soldiers on the War with Kurdish Guerrillas.* New York: Palgrave Macmillan.

Mathers, Jennifer G. 2006. "Women, Society, and the Military: Women Soldiers in Post-Soviet Russia." In *Military and Society in Post-Soviet Russia*, ed. Stephen L. Webber and Jennifer G. Mathers, 207–227. Manchester, UK: Manchester University Press.

Mayer, Jane. 2005a. "Outsourcing Torture." *New Yorker*, February 14–21, 106–123.

———. 2005b. "The Memo." *New Yorker*, February 27, 32–41.

———. 2005c. "The Experiment." *New Yorker*, " July 11–18, 60–71.

———. 2006. "The Hidden Power." *New Yorker*, July 3, 44–55.

Mazurana, Dyan, Karen Jacobsen, and Lucy Gale, eds. 2013. *A View from Below: Conducting Research in Conflict Zones*. Cambridge and New York: Cambridge University Press.

McKay, Susan, and Dyan Mazurana. 2004. *Where Are the Girls? Girls in Fighting Forces in Northern Uganda, Sierra Leone, and Mozambique*. Montreal: Rights and Democracy.

Moavani, Azadele, 2015. "For ISIS Women, Fraught Choices." *New York Times*. November 22.

Moffeit, Miles, and Amy Herder. 2004. "Returning Female GIs Report Rapes, Poor Care." http://www.sirnosir.com/the—film/resistor—84.html.

Moon, Katherine. 1997. *Sex among Allies: Military Prostitution in US-Korea Relations*. New York: Cambridge University Press.

Munn, Jamie. 2007. "The Hegemonic Male and Kosovar Nationalism from 2000–2005." In "Hegemonic Masculinities in International Politics." Juanita Elias, ed., special issue, *Men and Masculinities*, 10 (4).

Murphy, Evelyn, with E. J. Graff. 2005. *Getting Even: Why Women Don't Get Paid Like Men—and What to Do about It*. New York: Simon & Schuster.

New Profile. 2004. *The New Profile Report on Child Recruitment in Israel*. Ramat Ha-Sharon, Israel: New Profile.

Norton-Taylor, Richard, and Mohammad Alubedy. 2006. "British Alarm as Basra Erupts." *The Guardian Weekly* 174 (4): 1.

Office of the Inspector General, U.S. Department of Defense. 2003. *The Tailhook Report*. New York: St. Martin's.

Ogasawara, Yuko. 1998. *Office Ladies and Salaried Men: Power, Gender, and Work in Japanese Companies*. Berkeley: University of California Press.

Onishi, Norimitsu. 2006. "Japan's Likely Next Premier in Hawkish Stance." *New York Times*, September 2.

Oppel, Richard A. 2006. "Iraqi Accuses U.S. of 'Daily' Attacks against Civilians." *New York Times*, June 2.

Oza, Rupal. 2006. *The Making of Neoliberal India*. New York: Routledge.

Parpart, Jane, and Marysia Zalewski, eds. 2008. *Rethinking the Man Question*. London and New York: Zed Books.

Patten, Eileen. 2011. *Women in the US Military*. Washington, DC: Pew Research Center.

Peace Movement Aotearoa. 2015. "New Zealand National Action Plan on Women, Peace and Security: Preliminary Analysis." Auckland, October 23.

Pratt, Nicola and Sophie Richter-Devroe, eds. 2011. "Critically Examining UNSCR 1325," *International Feminist Journal of Politics*, 13 (4).

Puechguirbal, Nadine. 2003. "Women and War in the Democratic Republic of the Congo." *Signs* 28 (4): 1271–1282.

———. 2006. *Failing to Secure the Peace: Gendered Lessons from Haiti and Iraq*. Boston: Boston Consortium on Gender, Security, and Human Rights.

Refugees International. 2005. *Must Boys Be Boys?* Washington, DC: Refugees International.

Reichberg, Gregory M., Henrik Syse, and Endre Begby. 2006. *The Ethics of War: Classic and Contemporary Readings.* Oxford: Blackwell.

Rupert, James. 2015. "Sweden's Foreign Minister Explains Feminist Foreign Policy," Washington, DC: U.S. Institute of Peace, February 9.

Russella, Susan Garnett, et al. 2015. "The Legacy of Gender-based Violence and HIV/AIDS in the Postgenocide Era: Stories from Women in Rwanda." *Health Care for Women International,* August.

Saar, Eric. 2005. *Inside the Wire: A Military Intelligence Soldier's Eyewitness Account of Life at Guantanamo.* New York: Penguin.

Sands, Philippe. 2005. *Lawless World: America and the Breaking of Global Rules.* London: Penguin.

Sasson-Levy, Orna. 2003. "Feminism and Military Gender Practices: Israeli Women Soldiers in 'Masculine' Roles." *Sociological Inquiry* 73 (3): 440–465.

Sato, Fumika. 2012. "A Camouflaged Military: Japan's Self-Defense Forces and Globalized Gender Mainstreaming." *The Asia Pacific Journal,* 10 (3).

Scandlyn, Jean, and Sarah Hautzinger. 2015. " 'Victim/Volunteer': Heroes Versus Perpetrators and the Weight of US Service-members' Pasts in Iraq and Afghanistan." *The International Journal of Human Rights* 19(5): 555–571.

Schmitt, Eric. 2004. "Abuse Panel Says Rules on Inmates Need Overhaul." *New York Times,* August 25.

Schmitt, Eric, and David S. Cloud. 2006. "Military Inquiry Is Said to Oppose Account of Raid." *New York Times,* May 31.

Sciolino, Elaine. 2006. "Spanish Judge Calls for Closing U.S. Prison at Guantanamo." *New York Times,* June 4.

Seager, Joni. 2009. *The Penguin Atlas of Women in the World.* New York: Penguin.

Senate Select Committee on Intelligence. 2014. *Senate Intelligence Committee Report on Torture.* Washington, DC: U.S. Senate.

Shanker, Thom, Eric Schmitt and Richard A. Oppel. 2006. "Military Expected to Report Marines Killed Iraqi Civilians." *New York Times,* May 26.

Silva, Jennifer Marie. 2006. "Gendered Citizens, Gendered Soldiers? Reproduction, Resistance, and the Cultural Logic of Femininity." MA thesis, Department of Sociology, University of Virginia.

Singer, P. W. 2003. *Corporate Warriors: The Rise of the Privatized Military Industry.* Ithaca, NY: Cornell University Press.

———. 2006. *Children at War.* Berkeley: University of California Press.

Sitaraman, Srini. 2007. "Colonialism, Masculinity and Revivalist Hindu Nationalism: Communal Tensions and Weapons of Mass Destruction." *Journal of South Asian and Middle East Studies* 30 (2): 52–80.

Sjoberg, Laura, and Ann Tickner. 2007. "Feminism." In *International Relations Theories,* eds. Steve Smith, Tim Dunne, and Milja Kurki. London: Oxford University Press.

————, eds. 2011. *Feminist International Relations*. New York: Routledge.

Sjoberg, Laura and Sandra Via, eds. 2010. *Gender, War and Militarism*. Santa Barbara, CA: Praeger.

Solaro, Erin. 2006. *Women in the Line of Fire*. Boston: Seal Press.

Spees, Pam. 2003. "Women's Advocacy in the Creation of the International Criminal Court." *Signs* 28 (4): 1233–1254.

Sperling, Valerie. 2003. "'The Last Refuge of a Scoundrel': Patriotism, Militarism, and the Russian National Idea." *Nations and Nationalism* 9 (April): 235–253.

————. 2015. *Sex, Politics and Putin*. London and New York: Oxford University Press.

St. George, Donna. 2006. "Limbs Lost to Enemy Fire, Women Forge New Reality." *Washington Post*, April 18.

Stiehm, Judith Hicks. 2006. *Champions for Peace: Women Winners of the Nobel Peace Prize*. Lanham, MD: Rowman & Littlefield..

Stockford, Marjorie A. 2004. *The Bellwomen: The Story of the Landmark AT&T Sex Discrimination Case*. New Brunswick, NJ: Rutgers University Press.

Stockholm International Peace Research Institute. 2006. *SIPRI Yearbook 2006: Armaments, Disarmament, and International Security*. Oxford: Oxford University Press.

Strasser, Steven, ed. 2004. *The Abu Ghraib Investigations*. New York: Public Affairs.

Svedberg, Barbo, Laila Alodaat, Madeleine Rees, and Nela Porobic Isabovic. 2013. *Women Organizing for Change in Syria and Bosnia*. Geneva: Women's International League for Peace and Freedom.

Taber, Jane. 2006. "Making It Big in the Old Boys' Club." *Globe and Mail* (Toronto), July 7.

Taguba, Antonio. 2004. *Investigation of the 800th Military Police Brigade*. Washington, DC: U.S. Department of Defense.

Taira, Koji. 2003. "The Okinawa Factor in U.S.-Japan Relations," In *The Challenge of Change: East Asia in the New Millennium*, ed. David Arse. Berkeley: Institute of East Asian Studies, University of California, 273–297.

Tickner, J. Ann. 2001. *Gendering World Politics: Issues and Approaches to the Post–Cold War Era*. New York: Columbia University Press.

Turner, Karen Gottschang, with Phan Thanh Hao. 1998. *Even the Women Must Fight: Memories of War from North Vietnam*. New York: Wiley.

Ueno, Chizuko. 2004. *Nationalism and Gender*. Melbourne: Trans Pacific Press.

Urbina, Ian. 2015. "Tricked While on Land, Abused or Killed at Sea." *New York Times*, November 9.

U.S. Department of Defense. 2015. *Annual Report on Sexual Harassment and Violence at the Military Services Academies*. Washington, DC: U.S. Department of Defense.

Vine, David. 2015. *Base Nation: How U.S. Military Bases Abroad Harm America and the World*. New York: Metropolitan Books.

Ware, Vron. 2012. *Military Migrants*. London: Palgrave Macmillan.

Wayne, Leslie. 2006. "British Arms Merchant with Passport to the Pentagon." *New York Times*, August 16.

Weapons of Mass Destruction Commission. 2006. *Weapons of Terror: Freeing the World of Nuclear, Biological, and Chemical Arms*. Stockholm: Weapons of Mass Destruction Commission.

Weinbaum, Alys Eve, et al. eds. 2008. *The Modern Girl Around the World*. Durham: Duke University Press.

Weisman, Robert. 2006. "Colleges Craft Studies to Fit Defense Firms." *Boston Globe*, June 27.

Whitworth, Sandra. 2004. *Men, Militarism and UN Peacekeeping*. Boulder, CO: Lynne Rienner.

Wibben, Annick. 2011. *Feminist Security Studies*. London and New York. Routledge.

Women in Black. 2005. *Women for Peace*. Belgrade: Women in Black.

Women Living Under Muslim Laws. 2006. *Documenting Women's Rights Violations by Non-state Actors: Activist Strategies from Muslim Communities*. Montreal: Rights and Democracy.

Women of Color Resource Center. 2006. *Runway Peace Project: Fashion Resistance to Militarism*. Guide and CD. Oakland, CA: Women of Color Resource Center.

Women Waging Peace and International Alert. 2005. *Inclusive Security: A Toolkit for Advocacy and Action*. Washington, DC: Women Waging Peace.

World Footwear. 2014. "Footwear Giants Move Orders to Vietnam." http://www.worldfootwear.com. August 12.

Wright, Ann. 2006. "Women Involved in Prisoner Abuse: Perpetrators, Enablers, and Victims." In *Proceedings of the Conference Women in the Military Today, 19–20 May 2005*, ed. Lory Manning, 64–111. Washington, DC: Women's Research and Education Institute.

Wypijewski, JoAnn. 2006. "Judgement Days: Lessons from the Abu Ghraib Courts-Martial." *Harper's*, February, 39–50.

Zahedi, Ahraf. 2006. "State Ideology and the Status of Iranian War Widows." *International Feminist Journal of Politics* 8 (2): 267–286.

INDEX

ABOUT THE AUTHOR

Cynthia Enloe is Research Professor of International Development at Clark University in Massachusetts, where she has chaired both the Department of Government and the Women's Studies Program. She is the author of fourteen books, including *Maneuvers: The International Politics of Militarizing Women's Lives* and *The Curious Feminist: Searching for Women in a New Age of Empire*, as well as *Nimo's War, Emma's War: Making Feminist Sense of the Iraq War; Seriously! Investigating Crashes and Crises As If Women Mattered*; and a newly updated edition of *Bananas, Beaches and Bases: Making Feminist Sense of International Politics*. Her books and articles have been translated into Japanese, Swedish, Turkish, Korean, German, French, and Spanish.